MW00619630

How Does it Feel to Unlock Your l

I have high ambitions but I realized that I was at a turning point in my life. I was either going to be stuck at my limit of $65,000 per year or I was going to get, painfully, out of my comfort zone and make some serious changes. I have been blessed to work at a firm where my broker has given me industry-leading tools to succeed yet I felt frustrated, stressed out and full of anxiety. I have too many dreams and high hopes but I am stuck in the middle. I could not seem to apply what my broker provided me.

Then one day he sent me an email about a program called, "Efficiency By Design." Over the next several weeks, I was hit between the eyes and through the heart. My eyes opened to the breakthrough that was given to me. I learned with amazement as I was changed from within; I was equipped with the inner personal material that would equip me to cross the divide between those with above average success and those who fulfill their dreams, I'm now on pace to quadruple my income from the previous year… I was UNLOCKED!

Patrick Shamblin

This [efficiency class] is a huge opportunity for you to learn to keep those New Year's resolutions! I was fortunate enough to be able to go through the eight-week class and this has changed not only the way I think about my business but also the way I think about my life! If you feel you have room to grow in your business, this is the place for you!

Brooke Hengst

The Efficiency by Design program was truly a valuable tool to energize and streamline my business, and life, heading into the New Year. Darice's cooperative approach to education and coaching is so refreshing and easy to implement. By far the most rewarding class I have been a part of in years

Justin Knoll, 2010 President, Denver Board of Realtors

Please accept my sincere thanks for allowing my participation in the "Efficiency by Design" series. I must admit that I left the initial evaluation [the survey] with the belief that I need a major overhaul of my business practices. After attending the series, I have been able to adjust the critical areas and have seen tremendous results.
Many of the coaching series for our industry focus on the basics of a transaction or sales and marketing. This series concentrated on the business and productivity. That refreshing change would benefit most agents.

Because of your "Efficiency by Design" series, I have replaced the fear of not having the basic components of the business with the confidence and success of having a roadmap to accomplish my business goals. This simple change in philosophy has reenergized my passion for the business. Thank you!

Terry Wenze, 2010 Chairman, Aurora Association of Realtors

This profound information would benefit professionals in any industry with no limit on their level of success and it can be applied to any aspect of your life. She designed the tools and showed us how to apply them into our daily real estate practice. She taught us how successful professionals create their successful career actively, instead of creating it passively (waiting for their career to happen). She showed us how to actively direct, guide and participate in achieving a professional, successful career; instead of passively existing in it. I have been putting the systems and tools into place and have already seen the positive effects in my business. It just feels right!!!

Shelley Leyba Cale

I want to thank you for all the hard work and enthusiasm you displayed while teaching the Efficiency by Design classes. I am so grateful to you and really think that I have learned lots of things, which will help my business this year, and beyond.

Ann Corrigan

Your classes are exactly what I need! Its most things I have been aware of and it is helping clean out the junk in my head to get 'er done. I am still struggling with the whole family/business balance (I do not think that will ever go away); however, your classes are helping with that as well. I have made some changes and shifting duties around, thus giving me more RE/MAX quality time.

Being a new agent, I especially am grateful that you have included me in this group. I look forward to a successful career and working with you and your team. Thank you Darice! I appreciate and love your classes! Thanks for being there and helping me grow!

Denise Segura

I am finding Efficiency By Design a very useful resource. I would say as I am just setting up, my challenges are simple things like knowing what to do next for my business, etc. Your classes are helping me form good habits while I have no habits! So with your help, I currently feel I am just getting things moving in the right direction. Challenges for me are knowing what is going to be relevant in 60 to 90 days. I have no idea how much business I will be servicing, I have no idea which methods I'm going to be using most to generate new business, so for me at the moment I am working on 7 to 30 day goals.

Simon James

I am so super excited about you and these classes. I have been doing everything and loving the newfound tools. I want to thank you for doing this, as it has been a huge benefit for me.

Ashia Barela

The program is just what I was missing in my business :) I am a very structured person but what I was lacking was the set up to make my time work for me.

Emily Absher

I am fired up and ready to start an awesome week tomorrow! Thanks to YOU.... I am getting my old self back! Focused... driven... dedicated to making things happen. On my list (that is TIME BLOCKED, of course!!) I have a note to call you tomorrow.

Tami Pratt

I have been finding huge benefit in Efficiency by Design. As I mentioned in class today, I need a little more time to get it fully implemented and rockin' and rolling. I am finding the tools you presented to be critical in fixing some of my bad habits. For example, the time blocking is helping to keep me focused on what is important and when. The concept of separating out the Dollar Productive tasks, administration, and projects and planning are making a difference. The task tracker and hot sheet are going to be great too, once I really start using them. Just know that I feel I have been given many tools to make me successful in 2009 and beyond. Thanks for this.

Beth Erickson Sand

Working with Darice and her program has opened my eyes on so many levels. As a Manager, Business Coach and Broker Associate it has re-connected me to the things that I need to do every day to move my business forward. The class was a wonderful "jump start" the year and I recommend it to anyone who is looking to enhance their business.

Clara Capano, Sales Manager

Darice Johnston's program "Efficiency By Design" has helped me reorganize my business and my lifestyle. After making a huge shift in my business and my personal life, I need to reorganize my priorities. I recognized immediately that I only wanted to work during the "high dollar" hours, which meant I needed help. "Help" was not a word I used during my past 20 years. As I prioritized my goals, [doors] have steadily opened. Because I have set the groundwork and have the system in place taught in the program, everything is falling into place. I am able to handle it all with ease. With the help of Darice and the team I have surrounded myself with, I am loving this new lifestyle where a I am attracting more business daily. Thanks Darice!

Amy B. Cesario, Sales Manager

I have the great pleasure of being a Business Coaching client of Darice Johnston. She is a powerhouse of great ideas, a very gifted teacher and a true professional. Her love for teaching the "Business Organization System," which she has developed, makes it easy for students like me, to stay enthusiastically on track, follow my plan in a focused manner, prioritize tasks, people and events and be accountable for the progress I am making in achieving my goals. Besides, it is a lot of fun to work with her and I love her wonderful sense of humor! I recommend Darice Johnston without any reservations. She is an inspiration, a treasure to have in my life, and an absolute joy to know as a person!

Yvonne Rosnik, Branch Manager

Unlocked

Revealing the Eight Secrets of Highly Efficient Sales Professionals

Darice Johnston
Lon Welsh
Drew Shope
Bruce Gardner

Also by the Authors

The 2009 Guide to Colorado Real Estate Investing
Available Now
Lon Welsh, Charles Roberts, Michael Canon, Mike Welk

Thrive: How Realtors Can Succeed in a Down Market
Available Now
Lon Welsh, Bruce Gardner, Mike Welk, Drew Shope

The 2010 Guide to Denver Real Estate Investing
Coming 2Q 2010
Anthony Girard, Lon Welsh, Charles Roberts

Printed in the United States.

Editing and Layout Design by Drew Shope, Lon Welsh
Cover Design by Steve Bianco, ValInteractive.com
Back Cover Photos by Greg Murphy

For information to reproduce selections from this book, write to:

Permissions
Efficiency By Design, LLC
6834 S. University Blvd, #231
Littleton, CO 80122

First Edition
Library of Congress Cataloguing-in-Publication Data
Bruce Gardner, Darice Johnston, Drew Shope, Lon Welsh
Unlocked: Revealing The Eight Secrets Of Highly Efficient Sales Professionals/ Gardner, Johnston, Shope, Welsh
p. cm.

ISBN 978-0-615-34343-3

780615343

For the families of overworked sales professionals.
You are about to get your loved ones back.

Table of Contents

1. Introduction – Why We Wrote This Book

You were born to win. To be a winner, you must plan to win, prepare to win and expect to win.
Zig Ziglar

Lon Welsh
Founder, Your Castle Real Estate, LLC

I am one of the managing brokers at Your Castle Real Estate. We have six offices across metro Denver and we are the third largest independent brokerage in the region. I train and mentor many of the 200+ Realtors® on my team. I just completed a research project with some interesting things I think you will find to be very interesting: Sales people (not just Realtors) with strong efficiency habits make $206,000 per year, on average. Sales people with poor efficiency practices average $54,000. Amazingly, the highly efficient people averaged 46 hours per week at work vs. 38 hours for the inefficient people. This proves that making a high income in sales is not about working yourself to death. It is about working smart. In this book, *I am going to show you how you can make this transformation* in your own business. You will not need to become militant about organization skills to reap some significant rewards. You can implement many of the easier changes in less than ninety days.

Why did I do this research? About a year ago, the real estate market grew considerably more difficult. Many of my Realtors asked for advice on what they could do differently to succeed in a tough market. I did not have the answer. To learn, I launched a research project with business partners Bruce Gardner, Drew Shope and Mike Welk.

We sent a survey out to thousands of Realtors to discover what success drivers mattered most in this recessionary market. We were surprised that only about ten of our fifty ideas really mattered. To bring the ideas to life, we did one-on-one interviews with a hundred very high producers across the U.S. We asked them, "*What specifically did you do differently than your peers that lead to your outstanding level of sales success?*" The results of our findings appear in our previous book: *Thrive – How Realtors can Succeed in a Down Market.* Since its publication in April 2009, I have given dozens of workshops to discuss key findings and brainstorm how to implement the main ideas. I had two key learning points from the workshops:

1. Sales success drivers for Realtors also applied to sales professionals from other industries. ***All professionals in relationship sales face a set of common challenges.*** We can learn from each other.

2. We asked, "*What one thing would you most like to improve about your business?*" Naturally, sales people making below average income said they wanted more sales. However, sales people making above average income generally told us they were making enough money, but they did not have a life. All they did was work. Their family life suffered as a result. Even when they were at home, they were often thinking about work. This negatively affected their personal relationships.

In the summer of 2009, I took a series of efficiency workshops lead by Darice Johnston. I felt I had strong organization skills going into the class, but I learned several very powerful new lessons. I realized that Darice had the answer to the second finding from my *Thrive* workshops: *simultaneously achieving a balanced life and a highly successful sales career was possible with systems and efficiency.* Most importantly, it was apparent that her systems would increase productivity and sales effectiveness of disorganized sales people. As a managing broker of over 200 Realtors, I know **a lot** of disorganized sales people. Now, I can share tools with them to help them become more effective in reaching their dreams without compromising their time with family and friends.

I approached Darice with the idea of collaborating on a book to share her processes and ideas. Happily, she agreed. We began by utilizing the sixty-five question survey that Darice used in her efficiency classes to diagnose where attendees could most improve. In November 2009, we sent out these sixty-five questions in survey format to 12,000 sales people in industries related to real estate (Realtors, mortgage brokers, title insurance and property and casualty insurance brokers.) As with *Thrive*, the survey results proved that only a handful of the original questions made a measurable difference for income.

As you work your way through this book, you will be taking the short version of the survey. It concentrates on only the most relevant of the original questions. Then, we will reveal to you the eight key secrets of highly efficient **sales professionals**. You can use your survey answers to see how you compare to these efficient top producers. Your answers will serve as a guide in creating your ninety-day implementation plan.

The ideas in this book apply to sales people in all industries. We will show you practical, simple systems you can implement today to increase your income. Most importantly, we will help you get your life back.

Other than my introduction page located here, Darice wrote the balance of this book. She developed the original concepts and workshops. I did the surveys, provided amplifications to her ideas and helped develop the presentations… but the credit for this book is really hers. Accordingly, the rest of the book is Darice's first-person prose. I hope that you learn as much as I did. It greatly improved my personal productivity.

Lon Welsh, January 2010.

Darice Johnston
Founder, Efficiency by Design, LLC

I started my sales career in 2005 when an international title insurance company recruited me from their local competition. My sales team, who fondly referred to me as "The Rookie" because I had never "sold" anything, was well aware that my hiring manager gave me a sales opportunity because of my "charismatic personality." The reasoning behind his decision concerned me, to say the least. What if I was not as "charismatic" as they thought? What if I could not translate charisma into sales? At that time I was a single mother of two, and this position I was offered was a 100% commission opportunity. My dearest friends had frequently joked with me about how I have an innate ability to accomplish the impossible… but this was different. I had no sales experience. No inherited book of business. I was scared to death, but I was determined to succeed.

Even though I had never sold a product or service before, I had a strong aptitude for assisting sales professionals in accomplishing their goals. In my prior position, I had been hired for a very specific reason: to double the productivity of the company's sales team. My mission was to find a way to elevate the efficiency and sales effectiveness of very tenured sales professionals without the need to employ an assistant. The initiative was an exciting and challenging one. For nearly two years, I traveled between the company's branch offices, organizing the sales executives and helping them shift their thinking about how they used their time and how they processed their administrative work.

During that time, I created an effective time management system that *made* sense for sales professionals. (That says a lot, considering sales professionals tend to be repelled by systems, especially time management.) I also developed a simple, color-coded filing system for managing both paper files and digital files. Both techniques were unique, non-intimidating and easy-to-execute. I helped each salesperson to take the basic components of my system and personalize it to their unique needs. Upon executing the systems, many of these sales executives were able to double their productivity within a very short period of time. The results spoke for themselves. I had successfully assisted a tenured sales force to achieve greater sales results, simply by reducing their time and mental energy expenditure on their administrative functions… and they did it without hiring an assistant. This resulted in a substantial increase in the sales professionals' paycheck and a significant jump in the company's market share.

When I was approached by my current company, I had absolutely no idea how I was going to "sell" title insurance, but my intuition told me that selling title insurance was not what I was needed to focus on. Instead, I decided to direct my energy into creating relationships and providing my Realtor® clients with a distinctive value they would not find through any of my competitors. I determined that since my greatest natural gift was assisting sales professionals to amplify their sales by increasing efficiencies, I would position myself as an Efficiency Coach to real estate professionals. I spoke to anyone who would listen, and as it turned out, many people wanted to hear what I was saying.

That is when the magic started to happen.

It was easy for me to differentiate myself from my competition. While they were delivering coffee mugs and desk calendars, I was doing one-on-one consulting for my clients. I figured I could either spend an hour with someone chatting over a cup of coffee, or I could spend an hour helping them to develop and execute an action plan, design a marketing campaign or discuss unique business development strategies. My goal was to help them sell more real estate by deploying systems that "even a sales professional could love." The more real estate my clients sold, the more deals they brought to my title company, establishing a reciprocal 'win' for all involved.

In 2007, I took my consulting efforts to the next level. I assembled all of the tips, tricks and presentations I had used in my one-on-one appointments and developed two-hour long group coaching sessions. I drew on experience not just from working with Realtors and mortgage brokers, but also from entrepreneurs and sales professionals from other industries I had connected with. Class topics included time management, database management, organizational techniques, ninety-day action planning and marketing campaigns. I also shared some of the spreadsheets that I was implementing into my own sales business. **As the workshops progressed, it became more and more apparent that the materials I was teaching were not only in demand for Realtors, but for sales professionals in general** – especially those in industries requiring relationship-style selling. In 2008 I established my company, Efficiency by Design, LLC and began coaching and consulting sales professionals outside of real estate to successfully execute my efficiency systems into their sales business.

From personal experience, I can confidently declare that if you really want to run your sales business like a business, and sell more of whatever you are selling, you need effortless systems to support you in accomplishing that goal. Your systems need to help you not only build your business, but also balance your life. I am thrilled to bring what I feel to be a unique, simple yet powerful coaching system to sales professionals in all industries. It is my honor to continue to train my clients while I further develop this coaching program.

The greatest lesson that I have learned from my sales journey so far is this: my passion, when blended into my work, produces substantial results. Results that I could have not predicted. This exact concept is now a principle I teach to my clients: developing and living your Differentiating Point. As you blend what you are passionate about into your sales efforts, networking strategies and marketing techniques… the sky is the limit.

Darice Johnston, January 2010.

2. Why You Want What I Have to Give

Knowing is not enough; we must apply. Willing is not enough; we must do.
Goethe

Why is this coaching program different from any other? Let me paint a picture for you.

Have you ever participated in an expensive sales seminar or intensive coaching program? Perhaps a friend referred you. Perhaps a marketing piece caught your eye. Before enrolling in the program, you were excited about its promises. You thought, "This is just what I need to take my sales to the next level."

Once you made the investment and participated in the training, they *did* deliver the moon and stars. Your trainer was an absolute genius… charismatic, experienced and inspiring. You took copious notes, jotting down incredible realizations and unique sales techniques. With new hope and inspiration, you could not wait to get out of that convention and go increase your sales!

You headed home, anxiously anticipating the deployment of everything you had learned in the course. Your mind was racing with new ideas to implement, new approaches to take and new possibilities for your future, your finances and your family. Finally, you reached your office and sat down at your desk, ready to get started on building your new vision.

That was when you realized… you were back.

Back to…
- Stacks of papers on your desk, your credenza and your office floor.
- Hundreds of emails taunting you from your inbox, with more arriving right before your eyes.
- Sticky notes, multiple task lists and filing drawers heaping with "piles" instead of "files."

Suddenly, your feverish inspiration was doused with an ice-cold splash of reality. As you looked around your office, there seemed to be so much to do before you could even think about implementing anything you had just learned, and all of it seemed to be an "A" priority.

The creeping feeling of being overwhelmed took over your feelings of inspiration. The excitement from the seminar faded into the background. Within just a few days you found yourself, once again, stuck in the same old routine. Your significant investment of time, money and energy turned from inspiration into frustration.

Here is where I come in.

When you are ready, I can help you:
- Step out of the mire of disorganization that has been holding you back.
- Launch new systems of organization, efficiency and time management.
- Let go of old worn out habits, beliefs and self-limiting behaviors.
- Take responsibility for your work habits.

The beauty of my system is that it complements, rather than contradicts, every other sales, training, and coaching program. While the sales experts are teaching you how to sell more, I am teaching you how to become more streamlined, more organized and more efficient with your time, your space and your technology. I am here to supply you with key systems and thought processes to help you implement everything you have learned from everybody else. I work in concert with your sales trainer, your business coach and your sales manager.

I am your new best friend.

I am confident that regardless of whether you have been a sales professional for ten days or ten years, our work together is going to open your eyes. You will see the factual state of your business as it stands today in all of its glory… strengths, weaknesses and all. Then I will show you exactly how to make the simplest, most effective changes possible to launch yourself into a new level of success.

When I work with clients individually, I always start out by asking them how their business is doing. Many are feeling the pain and are honest with me about it. "This economy is killing me" is a popular one. I frequently hear, "I used to be at the top of my game... but I don't know what's happened." Others will put on their sales hat and start sharing all of the magical details of their marketing efforts, how great their networking is and about their various appearances in their community. I respond with, "That's great! How many of those activities have generated new business for you? How have your sales been in the last 12 months?" At this point, the conversation frequently takes a dramatic shift. Their body language changes. I know I have hit a sweet spot.

This is a common problem with sales professionals. We get excited about our projects, our initiatives and establishing ourselves as the local celebrity of our industries, but when we begin to examine the results we are achieving, things becomes very nebulous. Frequently we have either not measured our results, or inconsistency of prospecting and execution has hindered our results.

Do you see yourself in either of these scenarios? If so, feel good instead of guilty. You are not alone! It is common for us to dream, but not "do." I will help you change your focus. I will help you see clearly what is working, what is not working and how you can begin doing things differently to improve your results in your sales business.

I have great news… and not so great news. The great news is that you are personally responsible for the success you enjoy. The not so great news… is that you are personally responsible for the success you enjoy. Depending upon your outlook on your business at the time you are reading this book, that statement feels either really good or really bad. If you are feeling overwhelmed, then you will be less capable and less excited about being your own boss, making your own money and being 100% responsible for success. The feeling of being overwhelmed drives people out of sales careers. I am here to help make sure you can handle it all and still keep selling.

Your Multi-Faceted Business

When you step into the role of a small business owner and/or a sales professional, you are not just selling your product or service. You are operating an entire business, from A to Z. You wear many hats during the course of any given business day. Select a few from the list below that apply to your industry:

Marketing Coordinator
Event Planner
Contract Negotiator
Accountant
Operations Manager
Business Planner
Therapist
Transaction Coordinator
Publicist
Educator
Customer Service Manager
CEO
Friend

And, with honorable mention… sales professional.

Many sales people and small business owners are a one-person-show. It is not easy to juggle all of these responsibilities with limited (or no) administrative support. It is understandable that we can often lose sight of our end goal and forget that our main objective is to sell our product or service. Here are the three main problems that my clients experience. Maybe you can relate:

- So overwhelmed with the other responsibilities (to make your business work) that you run out of time or energy to prospect?
- Hiding behind these other responsibilities, using their need for your attention as an excuse to not get out there and sell?
- Only interested in selling? Do the other facets of your operations slip so dramatically that you jeopardize your business? Do you lose opportunities due to lack of organization?

Taking Control of Your Business

What if I told you there was a way for you to take control of your business, manage your time more effectively, deploy simple efficiency systems (without hiring an assistant) *and* attain the desired sales result you really wanted… all while maintaining a lovely degree of balance in your life? Would you believe me?

You should. Throughout this book, I am going to show you how.

The truth is that you can achieve all that you desire. You can attain the income, the balance and the success that you are inspired to attain. The answer lies in working efficiently, consciously and purposefully. When you work purposefully, you are taking control of your business. You run your business. Your business no longer runs you.

There are two main feelings we experience when business is not going well: feeling scattered and feeling overwhelmed. When you feel scattered, you have lost your sense of priorities. You have begun working by reaction instead of working purposefully. When you feel overwhelmed, you have so many incomplete tasks that your energy is drained before you even get out of bed in the morning.

Your sales success lies in your ability to be laser focused on what matters most… *at the time that it matters.* You must complete activities and tasks during the times when you can to maximize your productivity. In doing this one thing, you can eliminate feeling scattered and overwhelmed. I created my systems with this exact end in mind: to help you sell more efficiently while managing the operational side of your business.

In doing this work, I am not going to tell you, "Let's get organized first, and then you can start selling." At the same time, I am not going to tell you that your Tasmanian devil sales style is effective either. Either way, you lose opportunity. The first keeps you in the office and away from prospects. The second gets you out there, but I am going to bet that you lose half of your opportunities because you do not have effective systems to easily follow-up with prospects or to run your business efficiently.

You need both.

Since distractions can derail purposeful work, we will work on two tracks simultaneously:

1. Designing and executing systems of efficiency.
2. Developing new business and selling more.

Here is what you will experience by following the program in this book:

- Manage your time more effectively
- Jumpstart your personal productivity
- Realign your activity level with your desired results
- Elevate your efficiency and effectiveness
- Establish clarity of goals and associated tasks
- Create order and organization in your business
- Streamline your systems and processes
- Eliminate feeling scattered and overwhelmed
- Enjoy a greater balance between your personal and professional life

Most importantly, you will let go of self-limiting beliefs. You will begin to create new beliefs about success and your ability to attain what you most desire. This is an essential step in creating a new reality for your business.

* * * * *

In the next chapter, I will reveal *The Eight Secrets of Highly Effective Sales Professionals.*

3. Overview of the Efficiency By Design System

The reason most people never reach their goals is that they do not define them, learn about them or even seriously consider them as believable or achievable. Winners can tell you where they are going and what they plan to do along the way.

Denis Waitley

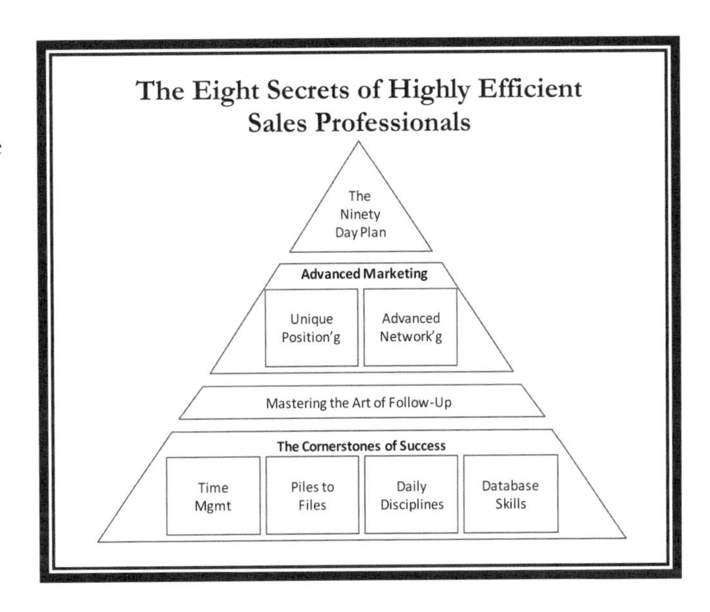

In the diagram below, you will see a visual representation of the Eight Secrets of Highly Effective Sales Professionals. It illustrates the relationship of the eight secrets.

There are four main components, starting at the bottom of the chart.

A. The Cornerstones of Success
B. Mastering the Art of Follow-Up
C. Advanced Marketing Techniques
D. The Ninety-Day Action Plan

Let's start our exploration of this coaching system by examining each component in more detail.

The Four Cornerstones of Success

The Cornerstones support the foundation of your business. The foundation holds together every operational element. You may already know from experience that if your foundation is strong, the rest of your sales business is operationally sound. Of course, the opposite is also true.

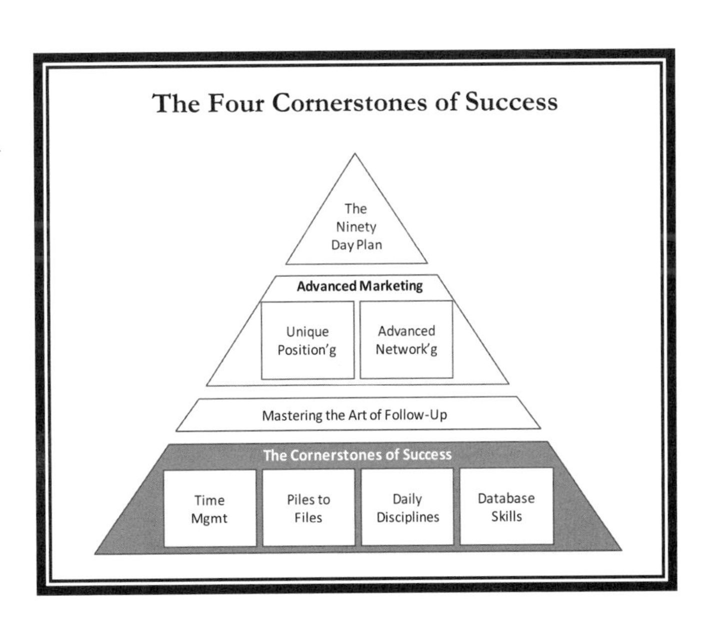

I refer to the Four Cornerstones of Success as the CORE of your business. CORE stands for an important acronym: **Center on Results Every day.** When you center (stay focused) on producing results in your business every day that means you:

- DO purposefully engage in dollar-producing activities during the key times of your day that bring about the greatest financial results in your business.
- DO NOT engage in (or get distracted by) any activities that can be "tabled" to a time of day that is best allocated to non-dollar producing activities.

Activity produces results. Perhaps I should sell this bumper sticker:

SALES activities produce SALES results.

Are you "very busy" every day but not producing sales results? That means that you are focused on activities that are not dollar producing. Does this describe you?

There are four cornerstones of success. They are simple systems that make your sales business work for you. They support you in staying organized, efficient and aware of where your next deal is coming from. This can be a difficult concept for the brand new salesperson to grasp. New people are inundated with sales training. You may struggle to grasp that CORE systems put in place now will save serious heartache later. Trust the millions before you who ran out of the sales gate with little preparation. Having a great sales presentation and thirty leads - but not having the database and the information into - results in lost opportunity after lost opportunity. Trust forefathers and foremothers. You need strong systems.

The Cornerstones of success are:

- Time Management
- Piles to Files
- Daily Disciplines
- Database Skills

The Cornerstones support the infrastructure of your business. Without them, you lose stability and momentum. The real beauty of the Cornerstones is that they bring you back to the basics. The most exceptional sales professionals are always very strong with the basics:

- They love strong habits and the daily disciplines.
- They are masters of how they use their time.
- They use their database to help them know where their next deal is coming from.
- They have the systems and tools to help them stay organized and execute priorities.

If your current sales are below your goals, or if your work/life balance is not where you desire it to be, at least one of your cornerstones is weak. You will soon take a survey to find out which one(s) need improvement.

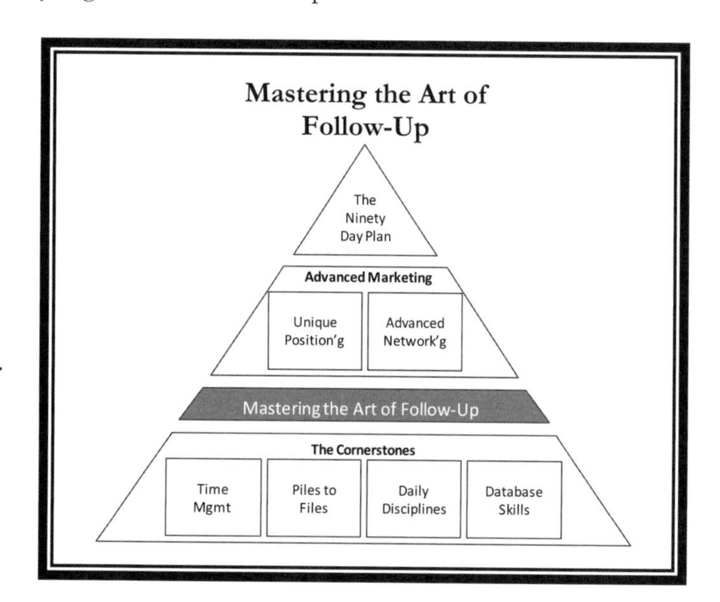

Mastering the Art of Follow-Up

The material in this book will apply to most industries. That is especially true of follow-up. In real estate, for example, the majority of Realtors obtain their sales from repeat business, referrals and relationships. Is this true in your industry? The survey in our earlier book, *Thrive: How to Succeed in a Down Market*, found that Realtors could expect to make about $800 to

$1000 per person per year with whom they have a good relationship. Separate research projects by both Larry Kendall and Gary Keller (geniuses in the real estate industry) found similar results. This implies that if a Realtor wanted an income of $100,000, they would need to have 100 to 125 people in their network with which they have a strong relationship.

The four Cornerstones will help you efficiently manage your day. As you progress with your career and ramp up your productivity, effective follow-up becomes increasingly important.

If you only have thirty people in your network, it will be simple to "stay in relationship" with all of them without an organized follow up system. It is a rare person who can manage this well with 100 clients without follow-up systems. It is quite impossible with several hundred people.

Advanced Marketing Techniques

There are some clear stages of career progress in some industries. For example in real estate sales, new professionals tend to market to their friends and family. In doing so, they do not necessarily need a unique selling proposition that makes them stand out from all of their competitors. This usually results in some sales, but usually at a relatively low level.

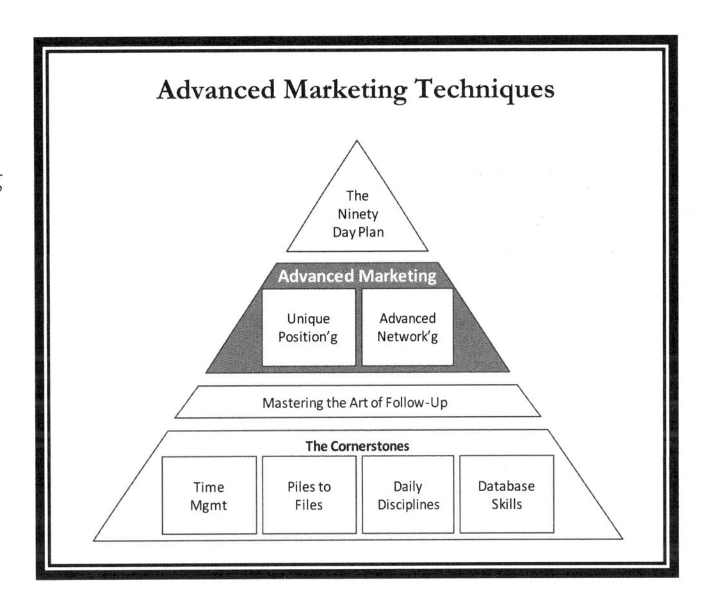

Usually in the second stage of their career, they will start networking within groups which they currently participate. Examples might include recreational sports groups, church groups, a local chamber of commerce or charitable organizations. Again, a unique value proposition is not essential, since the strong personal relationships are the basis for selecting the sales person over their competitors. Unfortunately, the number of possible sales within such groups is limited.

In the third stage of their career, the sales professional wants to grow their income beyond their friends and the groups in which they are strongly embedded. Attracting new clients beyond "the low-hanging fruit of current relationships" involves much more bare-knuckle competition. Clients will not choose them just because they have known them for years and are a good person. The prospective client needs a **compelling** reason to choose that sales professional over all of the choices, many of which are excellent. This book has two chapters to assist you if you are at that level of your sales career.

The first advanced marketing chapter, Positioning Yourself Uniquely, will help you craft a unique method of positioning yourself relative to your competitors. If you provide more value, you will attract more clients. The second, Advanced Networking and The Power Triangle, introduces some little-used networking techniques that are quite powerful. However, both of these methods assume you have already mastered the implementation of The Four Cornerstone Skills and the Art of Follow-Up. If you attempt the advanced marketing secrets before master the basics, your results will fall short of their potential.

The Ninety-Day Action Plan

Have you heard the saying that your outer world is a reflection of your inner world? This applies to your business, too. How your business looks and operates on the outside is a direct reflection of the time, attention, energy and clarity you have given to it on the inside. I will not ask you to plan your business ten years down the road. Instead, I will ask you to identify:

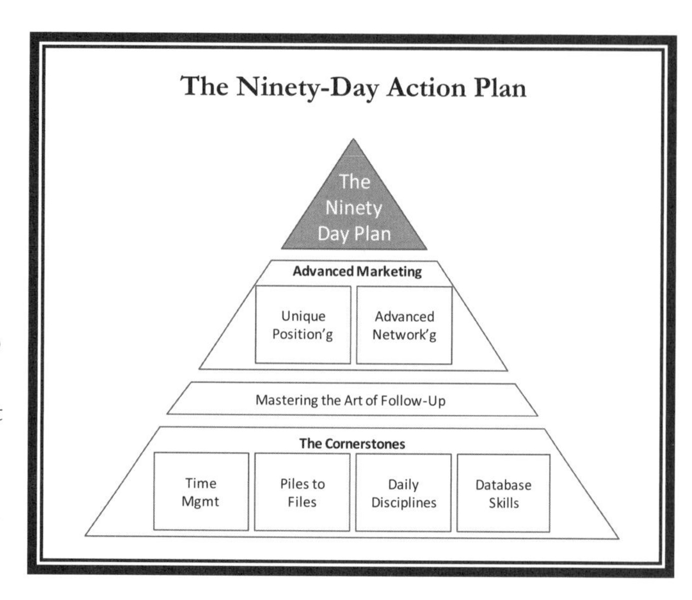

- The financial outcome that you desire within the next twelve months.
- The number of sales units you will need to sell to reach your financial goal.
- The strengths and weaknesses that currently exist within your business.

Once these three easy steps are complete, you will build a simple, non-overwhelming Ninety-Day Action Plan that you will begin deploying immediately. You will begin to experience life-changing results.

The Ninety-Day Action Plan will help you focus on activities that produce the greatest financial results in your business. Your Sales Manager helps you to define financial and productivity goals for the year. Your action plan will help you execute the tactical steps required to get ninety days closer to those goals. The shorter time horizon makes executing your plan and achieving your goals infinitely easier. Clarity matters: if your daily sales activity is undefined or ambiguous, your sales results will be undefined and ambiguous.

One planning tip: having a vision for your business is an essential part of its continued growth. However, the problem for some people is they become stuck in the planning process instead of getting out there and making things happen. They prefer planning over selling. You have to do both.

* * * * *

In the next chapter, you will take the short version of the survey to assess where your business is currently performing in each of these eight areas. If you want to increase your income and/or your free time you spend with your family, you are about to discover where to focus your efforts.

4. Assessing Your Business

In order to plan your future wisely, it is necessary that you understand and appreciate your past.
Jo Coudert

The state of your business today is the result of what you were thinking about and doing in the past. You can change your results quickly with some focused effort. I will help you to accomplish that.

Be very honest when you complete the following survey. I am a business coach, not a judge. Evaluate how your business looks today. Do not answer these questions based on how you would like it to be, or how you know it should be.

Answer the questions on the following pages. This survey is nearly identical to the one we sent out to 12,000 sales professionals in November 2009. We deleted the questions that ended up not being very helpful.

After you complete the questions in each section, add up your score. The top 10% of our survey respondents were put into the "A+" bucket. Below that you can see their average income (GCI = gross commission income). We put the next 15% into the "A" bucket (so, in total, the best 25% are A+ or A). The next 25% were assigned a "B"; the next 25% a "C"; and the final 25% a "D." You can see the average income for this group, as well.

In almost every case, the "A+" group made more than twice as much as the "D" group did. How do you stack up today? Where do you want to be in ninety days? Let's find out!

A. Time Mastery

1.1 – I feel comfortable with the amount of time I am spending on administrative tasks.	1 Strongly Agree — 2 Agree — 3 Neutral — 4 Disagree — 5 Strongly Disagree
1.2 – I spend at least 50% of my work hours on dollar productive activities and at least 25% of that time on new sales.	1 Strongly Agree — 2 Agree — 3 Neutral — 4 Disagree — 5 Strongly Disagree
1.3 – I am very good about performing only dollar productive activities during my most dollar productive hours.	1 Strongly Agree — 2 Agree — 3 Neutral — 4 Disagree — 5 Strongly Disagree
1.4 – I have adequate time for relaxation, family time, personal time and time to pursue my personal interests.	1 Strongly Agree — 2 Agree — 3 Neutral — 4 Disagree — 5 Strongly Disagree
1.5 – I am able to avoid needless interruptions during my workday and stay focused on what matters most in my business.	1 Strongly Agree — 2 Agree — 3 Neutral — 4 Disagree — 5 Strongly Disagree

Add up your points for the questions above. If you scored…

5-9 points: A+	10-11 points: A	12-14 points: B	15-17 points: C	18 or more: D
$171,000 avg GCI				$70,000 avg GCI

What do you think you are doing well?

____

____

____

What small changes do you think you could make that would quickly affect your business?

____

____

____

What larger changes would bring your career to the next level?

____

____

____

B. Piles to Files

2.1 – I have a system in place to track progress on current transactions as well as potential business.	← 1 Strongly Agree — 2 Agree — 3 Neutral — 4 Disagree — 5 Strongly Disagree →
2.2 – I have an effective filing system that allows me to keep clutter from my workspace. I easily find documents I need in seconds.	← 1 Strongly Agree — 2 Agree — 3 Neutral — 4 Disagree — 5 Strongly Disagree →
2.3 – I have a system in place to manage my email. I only tend to important and urgent email during dollar productive hours.	← 1 Strongly Agree — 2 Agree — 3 Neutral — 4 Disagree — 5 Strongly Disagree →

Add up your points for the questions above. If you scored…

3-4 points: A+	5-6 points: A	7 points: B	8-10 points: C	11 or more: D
$129,000 avg GCI				$65,000 avg GCI

What do you think you are doing well?

____

____

____

What small changes do you think you could make that would quickly affect your business?

____

____

____

What larger changes would bring your career to the next level?

____

____

____

C. Daily Disciplines

3.1 – I have tools and systems in place to help me stay on track with my daily, weekly and monthly priorities.	1 Strongly Agree, 2 Agree, 3 Neutral, 4 Disagree, 5 Strongly Disagree
3.2 – I pre-plan my day and my week before it begins.	1 Strongly Agree, 2 Agree, 3 Neutral, 4 Disagree, 5 Strongly Disagree
3.3 – I conduct my daily business using a schedule that works well for me.	1 Strongly Agree, 2 Agree, 3 Neutral, 4 Disagree, 5 Strongly Disagree

Add up your points for the questions above. If you scored…

3-4 points: A+	5-6 points: A	7 points: B	8 points: C	9 or more: D
$203,000 avg GCI				$56,000 avg GCI

What do you think you are doing well?

___

___

___

What small changes do you think you could make that would quickly affect your business?

___

___

___

What larger changes would bring your career to the next level?

___

___

___

D. Falling in Love with Your Database

4.1 – I maintain one database where I enter all of my contacts	1 Strongly Agree — 2 Agree — 3 Neutral — 4 Disagree — 5 Strongly Disagree
4.2 – I have a very clear way to qualify my prospects.	1 Strongly Agree — 2 Agree — 3 Neutral — 4 Disagree — 5 Strongly Disagree
4.3 – I maintain client records so I can capture customer preferences, important dates and record key information from conversations.	1 Strongly Agree — 2 Agree — 3 Neutral — 4 Disagree — 5 Strongly Disagree
4.4 - I update my database at least once a week with new names I have acquired to prevent "business card pile-up" and loss of follow-up.	1 Strongly Agree — 2 Agree — 3 Neutral — 4 Disagree — 5 Strongly Disagree

Add up your points for the questions above. If you scored…

4-6 points: A+	7 or 8 points: A	9 or 10 points: B	11 or 12 points: C	13 or more: D
$134,000 avg GCI				$51,000 avg GCI

What do you think you are doing well?

____

____

____

What small changes do you think you could make that would quickly affect your business?

____

____

____

What larger changes would bring your career to the next level?

____

____

____

E. Mastering the Art of Follow-up

5.1 – I set the appropriate number of appointments each week to reach my sales goals.	1 Strongly Agree — 2 Agree — 3 Neutral — 4 Disagree — 5 Strongly Disagree
5.2 – I know the number of new people I need to add to my database and marketing campaign every month, and add them.	1 Strongly Agree — 2 Agree — 3 Neutral — 4 Disagree — 5 Strongly Disagree
5.3 – I qualify potential customers using a needs-analysis approach. I do not waste energy on the wrong clients.	1 Strongly Agree — 2 Agree — 3 Neutral — 4 Disagree — 5 Strongly Disagree
5.4 – My past clients receive consistent communication from me on a regularly basis via social media, mail, email and phone.	1 Strongly Agree — 2 Agree — 3 Neutral — 4 Disagree — 5 Strongly Disagree
5.5 – I have a high-touch campaign to follow-up with people I have just met or clients who have demonstrated an immediate need.	1 Strongly Agree — 2 Agree — 3 Neutral — 4 Disagree — 5 Strongly Disagree
5.6 – I have a passive marketing campaign that I use to stay connected to past clients, as well as prospects who are not ready to buy just yet.	1 Strongly Agree — 2 Agree — 3 Neutral — 4 Disagree — 5 Strongly Disagree

Add up your points for the questions above. If you scored…

6-11 points: A+	12 or 13 points: A	14 to 16 points: B	17 to 19 points: C	20 or more: D
$136,000 avg GCI				$55,000 avg GCI

What do you think you are doing well?

____

____

What small changes do you think you could make that would quickly affect your business?

____

____

____

What larger changes would bring your career to the next level?

____

____

____

F. Unique Positioning

6.1 – I am pleased with the designations I currently hold or industry-specific training I have completed.	1 Strongly Agree — 2 Agree — 3 Neutral — 4 Disagree — 5 Strongly Disagree
6.2 – I stay up to date on market trends and understand how they affect my business.	1 Strongly Agree — 2 Agree — 3 Neutral — 4 Disagree — 5 Strongly Disagree
6.3 – I make sure my education includes sales training and professional training, as well as industry related and required training, to continuously improve myself professionally.	1 Strongly Agree — 2 Agree — 3 Neutral — 4 Disagree — 5 Strongly Disagree
6.4 – I have discovered how I can differentiate myself in my industry and my marketing efforts and products reflect that.	1 Strongly Agree — 2 Agree — 3 Neutral — 4 Disagree — 5 Strongly Disagree

Add up your points for the questions above. If you scored…

4-6 points: A+	7 or 8 points: A	9 or 10 points: B	11 or 12 points: C	13 or more: D
$138,000 avg GCI				$44,000 avg GCI

What do you think you are doing well?

____

____

____

What small changes do you think you could make that would quickly affect your business?

____

____

____

What larger changes would bring your career to the next level?

____

____

____

G. Advanced Networking

7.1 – I have established a polished and professional network of business partners. I feel confident referring my clients to them.	1 Strongly Agree — 2 Agree — 3 Neutral — 4 Disagree — 5 Strongly Disagree
7.2 – I regularly receive referrals from my business partners, referral partners and past clients.	1 Strongly Agree — 2 Agree — 3 Neutral — 4 Disagree — 5 Strongly Disagree
7.3 – I personally ensure that my clients receive responses to all inquiries, whether I am personally handling the inquiry or not.	1 Strongly Agree — 2 Agree — 3 Neutral — 4 Disagree — 5 Strongly Disagree

Add up your points for the questions above. If you scored…

3-4 points: A+	5-6 points: A	7 points: B	8 points: C	9 or more: D
$137,000 avg GCI				$62,000 avg GCI

What do you think you are doing well?

____

____

____

What small changes do you think you could make that would quickly affect your business?

____

____

____

What larger changes would bring your career to the next level?

____

____

____

H. The Ninety Day Action Plan

8.1 – I know the key things I must do daily, weekly and monthly to move my business forward. I do these key things consistently.	◄ 1 Strongly Agree — 2 Agree — 3 Neutral — 4 Disagree — 5 Strongly Disagree ►
8.2 – I have a clear vision and direction for my business that I am passionate about achieving.	◄ 1 Strongly Agree — 2 Agree — 3 Neutral — 4 Disagree — 5 Strongly Disagree ►
8.3 – I stay aware of trends occurring in my marketplace. My business plan is flexible. I can incorporate these changes into my business rather than feeling victimized by them.	◄ 1 Strongly Agree — 2 Agree — 3 Neutral — 4 Disagree — 5 Strongly Disagree ►
8.4 – I set annual goals for myself in writing and check progress on them at least monthly.	◄ 1 Strongly Agree — 2 Agree — 3 Neutral — 4 Disagree — 5 Strongly Disagree ►

Add up your points for the questions above. If you scored…

4-6 points: A+	7 or 8 points: A	9 points: B	10 or 11 points: C	12 or more: D
$114,000 avg GCI				$43,000 avg GCI

What do you think you are doing well?

____

____

____

What small changes do you think you could make that would quickly affect your business?

____

____

____

What larger changes would bring your career to the next level?

____

____

____

I. My Businesses Scorecard "Today"

Topic	Grade Today	Target Grade In 90 days
A. Time Mastery		
B. Piles to Files		
C. Daily Disciplines		
D. Falling in Love with your Database		
E. Mastering the Art of Follow-up		
F. Unique Positioning		
G. Advanced Networking		
H. The Ninety-Day Action Plan		

Where are your relative strengths? Are there some simple things you can improve in 90 days?

___

___

___

Where are your relative weaknesses? Are there some simple things you can improve in 90 days?

___

___

___

* * * * *

The average income of the sales professionals with an A+ "grade point average" (the top 10%) was $206,000. You might think they are working themselves to death. They are not! On average, they work 46 hours per week. The D players (the bottom 25%) earn $54,000 working 38 hours per week. This proves that it is not about working harder, it is about working smart.

- If you are currently a **C or D player,** we are not likely to get you to A+ status, unless you just had a major life change that gave you a big dose of motivation. It is much more likely that we will help you improve to a B. That would be a 45% increase in income. What impact would that have on your family – especially if you did not have to work any more hours to make it happen?
- If you are currently a **B player**, we can easily help you improve to be an A player. On average, you will make 27% more for your effort. It will be the easiest money you will ever make.
- If you are currently an **A player**, we can get you to A+ status with some fine-tuning. You will reap the biggest reward of all, a 105% pay increase: from $101,000 to $206,000, on average. You have always dreamt of being the top producer, and we will show you how to do it.

In the next chapter, we will see how you can use this book to make the improvements you need.

5. Getting Started

Reduce your plan to writing. The moment you complete this, you will have definitely given concrete form to the intangible desire."
Napoleon Hill

On-line Tools
Why the name, "Efficiency by Design"? Personally, I have never come across one organizational system that worked well for me in its entirety. I have always had to make revisions and adjustments to any product I purchased, which resulted in frustration and lost time. When I began to develop efficiency systems, I knew I did not want to sell them in a box or package, or create a product that could not be customized to fit my clients' needs. Instead, I wanted to create a *conceptual system – a system of thought rather than a system on paper.* Efficiency by Design is a result of that decision.

The following pages will reveal a number of different forms or "systems" that I have developed to help you apply the efficiency techniques suggested in each chapter. Every form I present in this book is available online. You can print these forms and use them "as is" or download and customize them to create your own unique, personalized efficiency system. You *should* personalize these systems to fit your unique style. They are not meant to be absolute requirements that cannot be changed. All of the tools that I use in this book and in my classes are intended to support your *thought processes* and how you think about organization and efficiency in your own business.

You can access these forms on my website, www.EfficiencyByDesignOnline.com. Please go online and register yourself as a member now, BEFORE you delve into each of these chapters. This gives you quick access to the "Members Only" page when you are ready to get started implementing the suggested tools.

The website will give you directions on how to contact me directly for more personalized coaching and assistance. It will also introduce you to products and services available through the Efficiency by Design community, which reaches well beyond this book to further support you in your efficiency journey.

How to Get Started
Review the "report card" at the end of Chapter 4, "Assessing Your Business." Initially focus on the four Cornerstones of Success:

A. Time Mastery
B. Piles to Files
C. Daily Disciplines
D. Database Management

Based on your report card scores, begin at one of the following four "points of entry."

1. If you ARE NOT at least at a "B" level on each of The Cornerstones, I would recommend you…

- Start with the chapter that helps you strengthen your weakest Cornerstone. If most of them need help, consider reading all four chapters.
- Skip the Follow-Up and Advanced Marketing chapters, and go directly to the Ninety-Day Action Plan. This is the last chapter of the book.
- Implement your plan.
- In ninety days, re-take the assessment.

- You might need to spend another ninety days on The Cornerstones. Invest the time. You will be richly rewarded for your efforts.
- In ninety days, re-take the assessment again.
- Move to the secrets that follow The Cornerstones only after you have the basics working well.

2. If you ARE a "B" or better on ALL FOUR of the Cornerstones, consider if there are a few "quick wins" in one particular Cornerstone that you can implement.

- A "quick win" is a simple change that you could make in thirty days or less that would improve your score in one particular Cornerstone, thus improving your day-to-day efficiency.
- Improving even one point (e.g., from "neutral" to "agree") is a measurable change and definitely worth pursuing.
- If you have some opportunities like this, select one Cornerstone and read that particular chapter first.

3. If all of your Cornerstones of Success are working well, consider moving on to the chapter Mastering The Art of Follow-Up. You should:

- Focus your time on Follow-Up skills before moving to more advanced topics.
- As with The Cornerstones, if you are at "B" level but see some opportunities for "quick wins," take the time to harvest them.
- Skip Advanced Marketing and complete your Ninety-Day Action Plan.
- In ninety days, re-take the assessment. Move to the advanced secrets of Advanced Marketing only after you have The Cornerstones and the Art of Follow-Up working well.

4. If you are the rare sales professional who is already proficient at all four of The Cornerstones, have mastered Follow-Up and seek to increase your sales to an even higher level, then the Advanced Marketing Techniques chapters should be your focus.

- You might still wish to skim the earlier chapters of this book. The small investment of time will likely be rewarded with some easy-to-implement ideas that will have a high payback relative to the time investment.
- Regardless of how successful you are, a proficient sales professional has a very strong grasp of "the basics," which are reflected in The Cornerstones. It is always great to review where you stand on these and make small adjustments as needed.

I am confident you will gain tremendous value from the ideas, techniques and concepts presented in the coming chapters.

Enjoy the journey!

6. Time Mastery

Time is what we want most, but what we use worst.
William Penn

The common person is not concerned about the passage of time; the man of talent is driven by it.
Schopenhauer

Time = life; therefore, waste your time and waste of your life, or master your time and master your life.
Alan Lakein

How Does Time Mastery Fit Into the System?
There are four Cornerstones of success. You do not necessarily have to master each of them to move on to the more advanced concepts. On the survey in the beginning of the book, you should be able to answer at least "neutral" instead of "disagree" on most of the Cornerstone questions.

This chapter will help you understand:

1. What do I need to do?
2. When is the best time to do it?
3. How will I "get it done"?
4. Implementation.

When you finish Time Mastery, you will progress to "Piles to Files," which builds on your skills.

Introduction to Time Mastery

Time mastery is the *one essential element* that provides you with a strong foundation for sales success. You get in your own way by allowing unimportant and non-productive activities distract you from our well-intentioned plans. Yet, time blocking is a touchy subject for some sales professionals. Many do not like it. However, the top producer down the hall knows it is essential to manage their time "on purpose." They are also disciplined enough to make it a top priority. After all, time is money.

For those of you who want to skip this chapter for fear of what I might ask you to do in preparation of mastering your time, I thought you would appreciate a list of what you will NOT be doing:

- Tracking how you spend every 15 minutes of your time in order to do some kind of painfully lengthy time study.
- Creating an inflexible schedule you "must obey" to be successful.

- Time blocking every moment of every day.

Some of you might think, "Darice, I have been told by many other coaches that I must do these (painful) things in order to manage my time. What else can you suggest that I do in order to achieve time mastery?" Let me tell you, as a sales professional myself, I know the challenges and the internal pushback that comes with implementing these types of solutions. That is why I am happy to tell you that I have an easier way.

How You Think About Time

Here are four very simple concepts we will cover. In this chapter, you will…

- DECIPHER what activities are dollar producing and non-dollar producing in your day-to-day processes.
- IDENTIFY what time of day is best for you to accommodate both types of activities.
- LEARN how to work efficiently.
- MASTER how to stay focused on what matters most... *at the time that it matters.*

> *"Self-discipline is the key with time management. The better a person can become at time management, the more that person will succeed. This is true in so many professions, especially in sales. Working hard and ensuring that I respond quickly to any item associated with clients is the key. Taxes and other personal matters need to be done late at night or early in the morning when you are not attending to client matters."*
>
> Quote from survey (Income over $100K)

My goals are to help you…

1. Gain clarity on efficiently managing your time (your most precious commodity).
2. Be inspired to establish new habitual ways of thinking about and protecting your time.
3. Provide effective tools to implement a time management plan.

Why even bother with time management? The answer lies in the graphs below. My experience with top producing sales professionals is that almost all of them have an organized way to maximize their efficiency. It enables them to spend time with their family when they finish working. They do not feel guilty and feel that they should still be at work or "on call." Less productive sales professionals tend to have a haphazard approach to time management. Naturally, their income reflects their level of discipline.

"I am very good about performing only dollar productive activities during my most dollar productive hours." Average 2009 Income.
Source: Your Castle Real Estate research

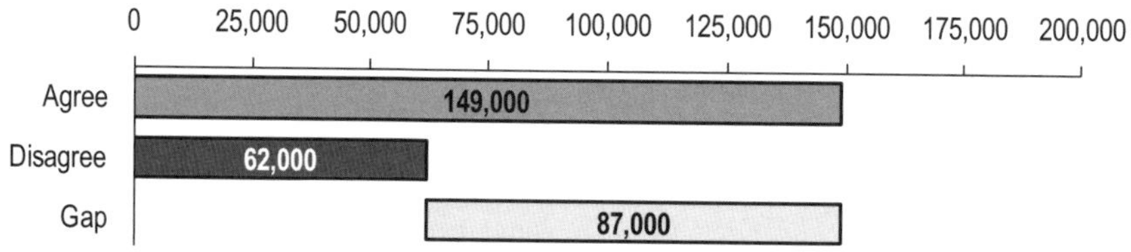

0 25,000 50,000 75,000 100,000 125,000 150,000 175,000 200,000

Agree 149,000

Disagree 62,000

Gap 87,000

Sales professionals who "strongly agreed" that they use their time efficiently reported 2009 income of $149,000. The sales professionals who "disagreed" reported income of $62,000. That is a big incentive to master your time!

To gain even better insight, we posed the question, "What is working well for you in this area?" Here are some of the comments we received:

- "I use my circadian clock to best advantage – I know when my higher energy times are."
- "I time block incoming calls."

- "Prioritizing and planning ahead (e.g., my appointments scheduled at least a day or two in advance when possible)."

The second question we posed regarding this survey statement was, "What challenges do you face?" Here were some of the comments we received:

- "I need to spend more time doing dollar productive tasks."
- "I have never thought of 'dollar productive' activities. I like the idea. Thanks."
- "I do not have texting on my phone. This helps me because I am not as distracted. I cannot be efficient with so many distractions... so I limit access. I answer as many phone calls as I can and return calls within two hours. I respond to e-mails 2-3 times a day."

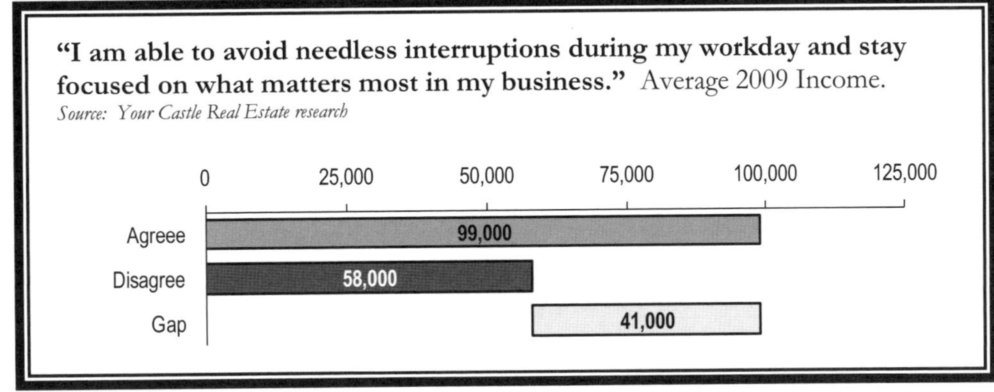

Regarding the "interruptions" question, "What is working well for you?" Here were some of the comments we received.

- "I manage to get 8 hours of sleep, which helps me be alert."
- "Time cannot be managed. I, on the other hand, have to manage myself." (Income over $100K)
- "I handle email only twice a day. I read for fifteen minutes every night right before bed... either something about organization, efficiency or attitude."

The second question we posed regarding this survey statement was, "Where are the opportunities for improvement?" Here were some of the comments we received:

- "Remembering that not everything is 'a must do!' I tend to treat silly calls as important because even though I know they are silly, the clients seem to think that the issue is important..."
- "Getting distracted with personal issues. The day goes by so fast that I do not have time to get everything done."
- "I work in an open office with five people. It can get very loud and distracting when everyone is in the office, talking and 'goofing off'. Staying on track with work and making the most of my work time can be very difficult."
- "Knowing when to quit work. When you own your own business in this tough environment... you are always working to try to get ahead."
- "Over-scheduling my time... not being as realistic as I need to be about time requirements for tasks."

> *"Simple time blocking allows flexibility but has structure. I plan to take a whole day off (at least one) every week." (Income over $100K)*
>
> Quote from survey; Income over $100K)

Distinguishing Dollar Producing Activity from Non-Dollar Producing Activity
We asked our sales professionals about their degree of focus on dollar productive activities.

The sales people who implemented this habit made three times more money than those that did not. What does habit YOUR schedule look like? Are you focusing on dollar-productive activities? How do these statistics affect the way you need to look at your own use of time?

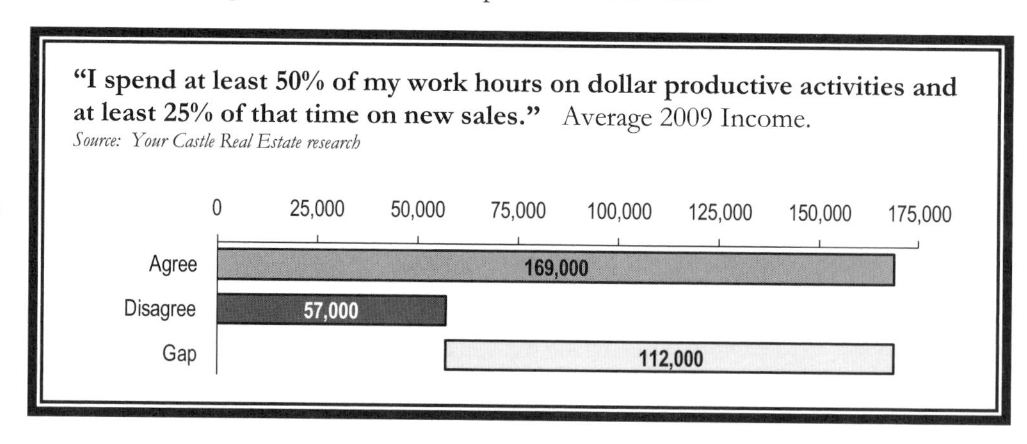

The Mastery System: What versus When versus How

To begin thinking of your time differently, you need to break it down into three questions:

1. WHAT do I need to do?
2. WHEN is the best time to do it?
3. HOW will I "get it done"?

Question 1: WHAT?

A man who dares to waste one hour of life has not discovered the value of life.
Darwin

Dost thou love life? Do not squander time, for that is the stuff life is made of.
Benjamin Franklin

Thinking through the WHAT of time blocking
To answer this question of, "What do I need to do? What do I focus my time on?" My system teaches you to structure your time mastery plan using five key elements. They are:

A. Dollar Producing Activities
B. Admininstrative Tasks
C. Projects and Planning
D. Meetings
E. Personal Time

You are now going to be building your customized Master Time Blocking plan. In my coaching and consulting experience over the last twelve years, I have been able to show most of my clients how each of their daily activities fit into these five time elements. This greatly simplifies the process of developing your Master Time Blocking Plan. Let's examine each element in greater detail.

A. Dollar Producing Activities

You know you are engaged in a dollar producing function of your business if your activity has at least one of these attributes in the text box. Examples:

- Prospecting for your sales pipeline
- Scheduling appointments
- Attending client appointments
- Lead follow-up
- Leads groups
- Social or business networking
- Entertaining
- Writing up contracts

Dollar producing activities are the highest payoff activities that you perform in any given day. When you examine the daily schedule of the highest producing sales professionals, you discover they spend at least 60% of their time on dollar-producing activities. Many of them actually spend close to 80% of their time on high pay-off activities. Their team, consisting of either an individual on their payroll and/or outsourced services, manages almost everything else required for day-to-day business.

Ok… so I just felt your resistance as you read that last sentence about a top producer's "team." I can hear it already, "Darice, I do not have the money to pay someone else to assist me." However, if you are at a point where you cannot seem to grow past a certain net income, you absolutely must consider the following equation: Determine how much money you can make per hour if given the opportunity to focus on dollar-producing activities. Then, determine how much money you would pay someone else per hour to assist you, even if it is part-time assistance, or outsourcing one or two tasks. This equation will very clearly reveal to you that while you feel you "cannot afford" to pay someone for assistance, the TRUTH is that if you are ready to step it up a notch, you can simply no longer afford to "do it all yourself.."

Attributes of Dollar-Productive Activities:

- Results-driven
- Involves face time (appointments with a current client or a qualified prospect)
- Voice time to maintain relationships with your clients and prospects or to schedule appointments
- Activity driven (activity produces results) (e.g., attending a networking event to meet new prospects)

Think it through… for YOU

Take a moment to jot down some of the dollar productive activities that are part of your typical month:

____________________ ____________________

____________________ ____________________

____________________ ____________________

Ask yourself these questions:

- Are there any activities for which I would like to allocate more time? Less time?
- Which ones provide the most value to my overall business? Least value?
- Do I excel at these activities or can I delegate them?
- To whom would I delegate these activities? What person, company or service can assist me?

B. Administrative Tasks

You know you are engaged in an Administrative function of your business if your activity has at least one of the attributes in the text box. Administrative tasks are "low leverage." They are the lowest pay-off activities that you accomplish in any given day. Yes, they are important. Yes, they must be done by someone, but they do not have to be done by you. As your business grows, they are the first candidates for outsourcing. My goal is to help you minimize the time you spend on administrative so you can maximize dollar productive and personal time.

Attributes of Administrative Activities:

- Task driven and/or on-going (e.g., sending out a monthly newsletter)
- Current business (once the contract is signed)
- Has the potential to be outsourced

What financial impact could this have on your business?

OUTSOURCE. This is an important enough point for me to reiterate. Delegate and outsource absolutely anything you possibly can if you want to take your sales to the next level. The reason our top producing sales professionals are "comfortable with the amount of time they are spending on administrative tasks" is that they are not doing very many of them. They delegate the majority of these tasks to someone else or find services that help them execute these tasks more efficiently.

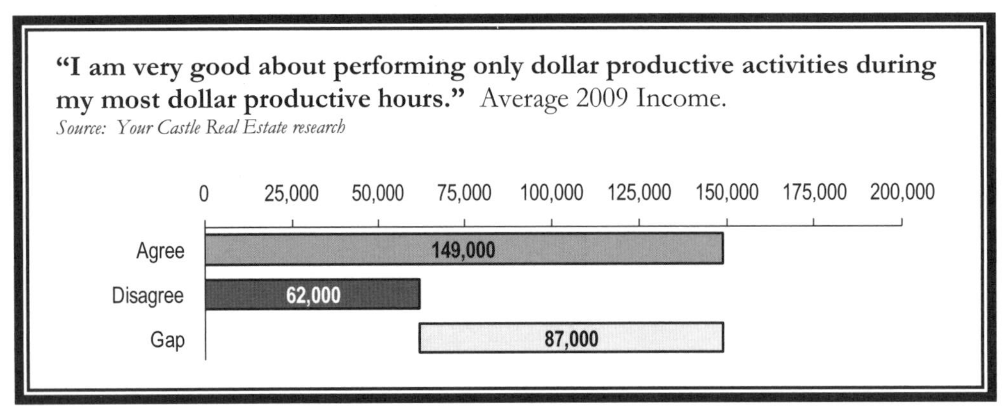

An interesting fact: Did you know that if you worked for one additional hour every day you would add six more forty-hour workweeks to your schedule every year? This illustrates how much of your dollar productive time to stolen when you perform low value tasks.

Think it through… for YOU

Take a moment to jot down some of the low-leverage administrative tasks that are part of your typical month:

____________________________ ____________________________

____________________________ ____________________________

____________________________ ____________________________

Ask yourself these questions:

- Are there any for which I would like to allocate more time? Less time?
- Which tasks provide the most value to my overall business? The least value?
- Which tasks are candidates for outsourcing?
- To whom would I delegate these activities? What person, company or service can assist me?

C. Projects and Planning

You know you are engaged in a Projects or Planning function of your business if your activity includes at least one of the following attributes in the text box. Examples:

- Long term or strategic planning
- Planning for next week
- Accounting
- Cleaning up your email box
- Updating up your database
- Assembling your presentations
- Planning client events
- Setting up efficiency systems

I generally define a project as something that takes longer than thirty minutes to complete. Execute projects during your "project and planning" time block. Anything taking less than thirty minutes is an administrative task, which you would execute during your "administrative" time block.

> **Attributes of Project and Planning Activities:**
>
> - Has a scheduled beginning and an end
> - Requires research
> - Is creative
> - Is strategic

Projects are rarely high pay-off activities in and of themselves, but they can lead to high pay-off results. Let's look at two high-value examples to bring this to life:

- In a later chapter, we will discuss what you do to differentiate your service from your competitors. DEVELOPING differentiated services in your business would be time blocked as "project" time in your calendar.
- In a different chapter, we discuss the importance of having a clear ninety-day action plan for your business. The time it will take you for to DEVELOP your plan would be time blocked as "planning" time in your calendar.

Low-value examples of projects would include accounting and organizing. While these kinds of projects support your execution of high pay-off activities, in and of themselves they do not necessarily lead to high pay-off results.
Low production sales people often "hide behind" or "get stuck inside" of projects and planning.. These activities keep them so "busy" they find themselves without an adequate amount of time to sell.

Think it through… for YOU
Take a moment to jot down some of the project and planning tasks you have worked on in the last year:

______________________________ ______________________________

______________________________ ______________________________

______________________________ ______________________________

Ask yourself these questions:

- Are there any for which I would like to allocate more time? Less time?
- Which ones provide the most value to my overall business? The least value?
- Are there any elements to these projects that are candidates for outsourcing?
- To whom would I delegate these activities? What person, company or service can assist me?
- Are there projects I suspect would be high value that I have not done… perhaps due to lack of time?

D. Meetings

How much of your time do you spend in meetings? Which of those meetings should you continue to engage in? For the sake of setting up your time management plan, I am asking you to note only professional, regularly held meetings or standing appointments. Examples:

- Sales meetings
- Marketing meetings
- Chamber meetings
- Leads groups
- Board meetings
- Volunteer activities

Be careful with meetings. Some regularly reoccurring meetings are mandatory, such as with your sales manager or executive teams. You cannot avoid all low pay off meetings. Try to make these as efficient as possible. However, other meetings *appear* to be high pay off opportunities when in fact they turn in to low pay off commitment nightmares. It is easy to get lost inside of serving on boards, volunteer activities or leads groups. How effective these meetings are is really up to you. How many meetings you are attending? How many boards are you serving? How many leads groups bring you value? Take an honest look at how those meetings are actual incubators for new business. If the original intent with these meetings was to gain visibility for your sales businesses but those meeting are not paying off, cut them out of your schedule and make room for a more productive use of your time.

Take a moment to jot down some of the meetings that are a part of your typical month:

________________________ ________________________

________________________ ________________________

________________________ ________________________

Ask yourself these questions:

- Are there any for which I would like to allocate more time? Less time?
- Which ones provide the most value to my overall business? The least value?
- What would happen if I eliminated the least valuable meetings?
- What can I do to streamline any one or more of these meetings?

E. Personal Time

Your time management plan should reflect any personal meetings, personal time you give to yourself as well as consistent family responsibilities. These would include:

- Regularly scheduled family time
- Standing personal appointments
- Personal time for self-care such as exercising regularly
- Desired time; time that you want to include (e.g., golf, meditation, hobbies)

Think it through… for YOU
Take a moment to jot down some of the personal time activities that are part of your typical month:

____________________________ ____________________________

____________________________ ____________________________

____________________________ ____________________________

Ask yourself these questions:

- Are there any for which I would like to allocate more time? Less time?
- Which activities are the most valuable? Least valuable?
- What would it mean for my happiness if I could increase the time spent on these activities by 10%? 25%?

If you are looking to increase your personal time and leverage your time spent on work, here are a few examples of what you can do to get some assistance for personal items for little extra money:

- Dry Cleaning delivery
- Online shopping
- Online banking
- Accounting services

What other services can you take advantage of?

____________________________ ____________________________

____________________________ ____________________________

____________________________ ____________________________

Question 2: WHEN?

Do not be fooled by the calendar. There are only as many days in the year as you make use of. One man gets only a week's value out of a year while another man gets a full year's value out of a week.
Charles Richards

The key is in not spending time, but in investing it.
Stephen R. Covey

Ordinary people think merely of spending time. Great people think of using it.
Unknown

Thinking through the WHEN of time blocking.
Examine what currently works for you and what needs to be changed. *This is an essential element to your continued success.* Systems that force a sales professional into a box, or require performing specific activities during specific time slots can be a dangerous cocktail for rebellion. After all, we are easily distracted creatures who enjoy freedom and flexibility. If we loved absolute structure, we would get a desk job.

In our survey we found working with a schedule that works well for us as individuals really improves the income earned by sales professionals.

"I conduct my daily business using a schedule that works well for me."
Average 2009 Income.
Source: Your Castle Real Estate research

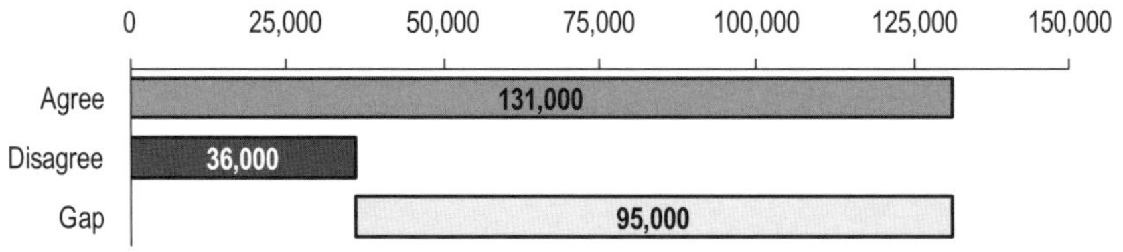

0 25,000 50,000 75,000 100,000 125,000 150,000

Agree	131,000
Disagree	36,000
Gap	95,000

Regarding this survey statement, we posed the question, "What is working well for you?" Here were some of the comments we received:

- "Time blocking helps a lot."
- "Daily exercise and meditation help me keep the craziness in proportion."

The second question we posed regarding this survey statement was, "What challenges do you face?" Here were some of the comments we received:

- "Getting bogged down with things that come up on particular deals instead of achieving the goals I had set for myself that day or week." (Income over $100K)
- "Working at home presents me with interesting alternatives to staying on track, especially with something I do not enjoy."
- "Following my plan rather than getting pulled into crisis management." (Income over $100K)
- "Time management with work and young kids."
- "Staying on task when working with multiple clients. It is easy to get side tracked."

"I am usually in the office at least one hour before anyone expects me, so that I can get the emails and non-productive calls taken care of and out of the way."

Quote from the survey

- "The constant changes in the plans - not allowing enough time per item." (Income over $100K)
- "Wake up early! It works every time." (Income over $100K)

Let's consider an example for a sales professional who focuses on selling title insurance policies to Realtors®. In most industries, Monday to Friday from 8AM to 5PM are the general working hours, but 9AM to 3PM often seems to be better for reaching Realtors. This is because many of the Realtor's clients have 9 – 5 jobs. Their clients will leave work a little early to look at properties (during the week) between 3 – 7PM. Thus, after 3PM on weekdays it can be difficult to reach high-production Realtors. Since many of these Realtors work late into the day, they often do not start work at 8AM. Many work between the hours of 10AM – 6PM.

When attempting to connect with Realtors, Tuesday, Wednesday and Thursday are more effective days than are Monday and Friday. Many Realtors work much of the weekend showing homes to clients and taking new listings. Since they work many hours on the weekends, many Realtors take Monday off when they can. Many of the Realtors working on Mondays are processing the listings they took over the weekend, writing contracts for homes shown to buyers on the weekend, or managing offers that they received on their listings over the weekend. Monday tends not to be a good day to reach Realtors. Busy Realtors often spend Fridays preparing for their weekends with clients.

> **Dollar Productive Time**
>
> For many sales professionals, identifying answers to these questions is pure revelation. In general, their prospecting approach (and timing) is not well defined. If this describes your current situation, you should expect haphazard results. Highly productive sales professionals know when their future clients are most likely to be receptive to prospecting calls, meetings and events. They reserve these times on their schedule for these essential dollar productive activities.

To summarize, for title insurance sales professionals to reach Realtor prospects, there are 18 "prime time hours" each week that are the most desirable: 9AM-3PM on Tuesday, Wednesday and Thursday. There are also "shoulder times" that are good for prospecting, but not quite as good as the prime time hours. Those might be 9AM-3PM on Monday and Friday. That is another 12 hours. The rest of the hours in the week might be the least productive from a prospecting viewpoint. Allocate the less productive hours to projects, planning or administrative functions. An efficient title insurance professional would.

Think it through… for YOU
When are the key dollar productive times for your industry? For the type of client you would most like to target? Take a moment to think of which days are most effective, and the reasons for this:

____

____

____

What times are most effective (prime time)? What times are a little less effective (shoulder time)? What times are ineffective?

____

____

Do you have different client segments that might need different communication methods (calls, in-person, texting, Facebook)?

You should deliberately schedule lower value administrative and project work during the dollar UNproductive times of the week. This simple change will dramatically improve the efficiency and effectiveness of your prospecting. By doing so, you will work the same number of hours while increasing your income. Alternatively, you can choose to maintain your current income and greatly reduce your prospecting time.

"I use a home office. I love to be around other sales professionals and our staff. When I go into the office, it is a real time-drainer. I learned a long time ago, as much as we all like each other, no one there is going to buy anything from me." (Income over $100K)

Quote from the survey

This is both the art and science in this next exercise. If you have never thought about this before, it will take an educated guess to get started. That is fine. Do your best. Track your results. Because you are now aware of the concept, you will notice many time management opportunities things that you were not aware of in the past. Make an appointment with yourself in two weeks to update your estimations of the most effective times. Over time, your "prime time" slots will become more and more accurate.

Another way to figure this out is to talk with some existing clients that have a profile similar to the type of clients you would like to attract. Ask them about the rhythm of their days and weeks to get a sense of their schedule.

Here is a worksheet to help you focus your thoughts. When answering these questions, take into consideration the time of day and the days of the week, when you are BEST ABLE to accomplish these items IN THE MOST EFFICIENCT AND PRODUCTIVE WAY.

Daily Prep & Completions/Deliverables

What time of day is the quietest when you can concentrate without interruption on "setting up" your day?

____

What time of day do you feel you are "winding down" from working and ready to tie up loose ends?

____

Current Client Files & Connecting with Current Clients

What time is best suited for you to be available for handling current client files?

____

What time of day, or days of the week is best to call and check in with your current clients to provide them with updates, etc.

____

Projects, Marketing and Long Term Planning

What time, or day of the week, do you feel you have the most number of quiet, concentrated hours?

____

Dollar Producing Activities

What time of day do you feel most energized?

____

What time of day, or day of the week, do you get the best results from making phone calls?

____

What activities are you involved in that allow you visibility and exposure to new people?

____

How many appointments do you want to have with prospective clients every week, and what days and times do you want to accomplish this?

____

What evenings are you willing to work late to meet with clients?

____

What hours during the weekend are you willing to spend on generating new business?

____

Personal Time & Family Relationships

What times of day do you (or would you like to) enjoy self-care activities such as exercising, yoga, walking and meditation?

____

What times of day, and days of the week, do you have family or relationship obligations and consistent plans?

____

We will use your answers in the next section when we build your time graph.

Question 3: HOW?

Make use of time, let not advantage slip.
Shakespeare

This time, like all times, is a very good one, if we but know what to do with it.
Emerson

Thinking through the HOW of time blocking.
I will open this segment of the chapter with a quote from one of the most powerful time mastery articles of have ever read. This is an excerpt from the article, Time Mastery by Dirk Zeller, President & CEO of Real Estate Champions.

> *"You must win the game of distraction. We all have distractions daily. It is what we DO with the distractions that come our way that matters. The difference between a time waster and a time master is THE LENGTH OF TIME IT TAKES FOR THAT PERSON TO GET BACK ON TRACK. For a time waster, it could be hours, or even days, to get back on track. For a time master, it will be minutes before they are back on track. PEOPLE WHO CONTROL TIME EARN MORE MONEY."*

My goal with this chapter is to help you *control your time* and *earn more money*. Your tool is the Time Mastery Graph. After you have built this graph, you will have an accurate picture of the best times of day and the best days of the week for you to execute dollar productive activities, administrative tasks, and projects. You will also have a picture of the times and days that you can enjoy – guilt free – quality personal time.

In Living Color – Your Personalized Time Mastery Graph
It is time for you to begin building your personal time management system in living, breathing color. You will find that my entire efficiency coaching system is dependent upon the first four weeks of this course, which tie to chapters six, seven, eight and nine of this book. Time Mastery is the chapter that kicks all of that off. The colors designated to specific activities on your Time Mastery Graph will be woven throughout your entire efficiency system. Color brings all of the necessary elements of your efficiency system to life.

> *"Knowing what type of person I am. I work better and clearer in the morning, so critical tasks I perform then."*
>
> Quote from the survey

In the next several pages, I will be giving you the information you need to create your own personalized Time Mastery Graph. I want to encourage you to let go of any previously held beliefs about time management process. If you look at this with an eye for intimidation, you will find it intimidating. It is not. Just walk through everything I tell you, step by step, and you will come out on the other side of this process victorious. You will have achieved greater clarity of HOW to use your time and have renewed energy to hit the ground running.

Building Your Personalized Graph
You are going to build your graph by walking through an exercise. First, you will identify how much of time you allot to two specific activities: personal time and meeting time. By examining these first, you can begin to make necessary adjustments in your use of time. Here is what you will need to begin this exercise:

1. Gather highlighters in the following colors: green, blue, purple, orange and yellow
2. Go to: www. EfficiencyByDesignOnline.com to download your time blocking forms. I suggest you print five copies to represent five weeks of the month. Simply register on the site and you will immediately receive a

user name password to access the MEMBERS ONLY page. Below is a sample of the form you will be downloading:

ORANGE – PERSONAL TIME

You will start building your time management graph with Orange, which represents your Personal Time.

Using the template available from my website, fill in with your orange highlighter the times of day and days of week you have personal commitments and family obligations. Color in blocks of time that you have family responsibilities, personal appointments, when you need to be available for children after school, etc. Make sure that you have included time for yourself in your "personal" time. Many of you parents out there may have family time carved out in their graph perfectly… but remember to schedule in time for yourselves, too. Consider time with friends, hobbies, exercising, etc.

Time Blocking - A Sample Weekly Snapshot

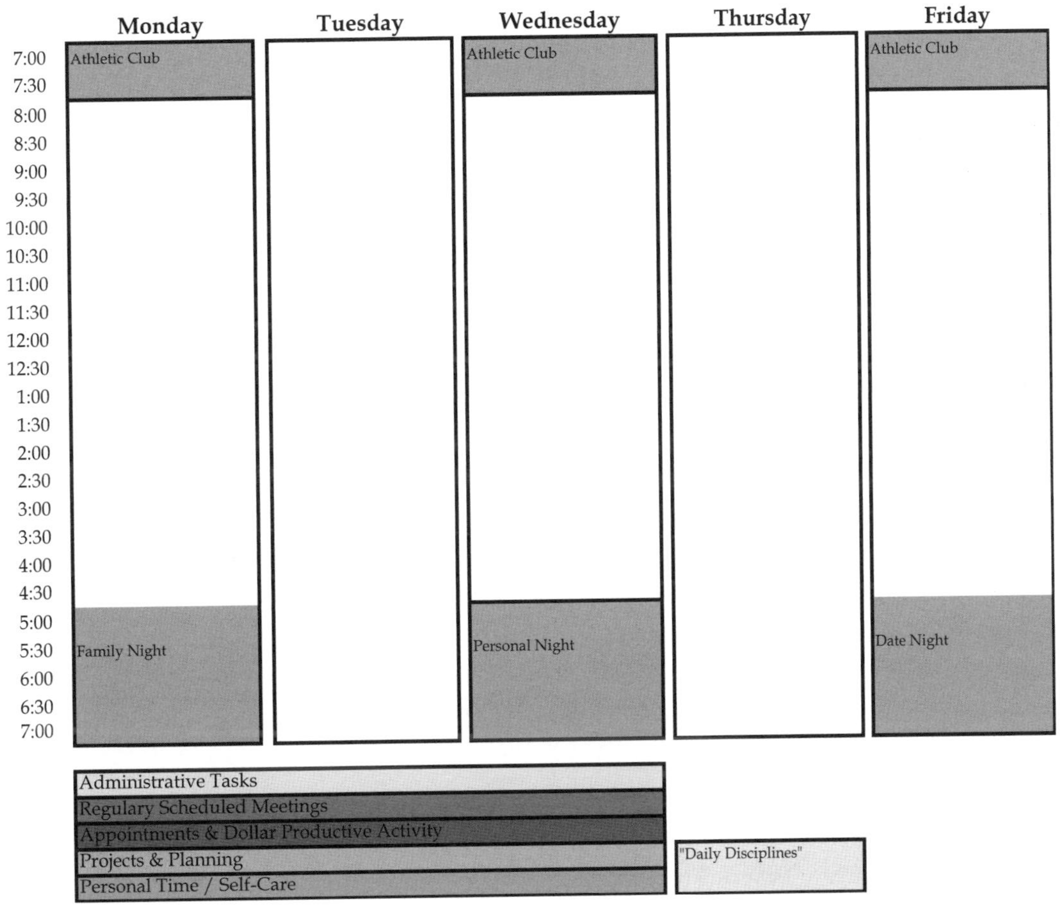

Monday Tuesday Wednesday Thursday Friday

7:00 7:30 8:00 8:30 9:00 9:30 10:00 10:30 11:00 11:30 12:00 12:30 1:00 1:30 2:00 2:30 3:00 3:30 4:00 4:30 5:00 5:30 6:00 6:30 7:00

Athletic Club
Athletic Club
Athletic Club
Family Night
Personal Night
Date Night

Administrative Tasks
Regulary Scheduled Meetings
Appointments & Dollar Productive Activity
Projects & Planning
Personal Time / Self-Care

"Daily Disciplines"

Note for your actual time graph, you will want to include Saturday and Sunday, too.

BLUE – REOCCURING PROFESSIONAL MEETINGS
The next color you will fill in is Blue, which represents standing professional appointments and reoccurring business meetings.

Now indicate with your blue highlighter when your regularly scheduled/reoccurring meetings or standing professional appointments are. Examples include sales meetings, marketing meetings and mastermind groups.

Time Blocking - A Sample Weekly Snapshot

	Monday	Tuesday	Wednesday	Thursday	Friday
8:00					8:00 Marketing Mtng.
8:30			Broker Opens &		
9:00			Property Previews		
9:30					
10:00					
10:30			Offi ce Meeting		
11:00					
11:30					
12:00					
12:30					
1:00					
1:30					
2:00					
2:30					
3:00					
3:30					
4:00					
4:30					
5:00					
5:30	Family Night		Personal Night		Date Night
6:00					
6:30					
7:00					

Now…STOP!

Examine what you see in front you. It is probably very revealing. Now that you have colored in the personal obligations and professional meeting times that are REQUIRED of you (or that you have committed to), you can better see the days and times you have available to complete sales activities, administrative process and project and planning time for your business.

Do you see a healthy amount of orange? If you are an at-home parent and need to take a lot of time for your family, you may find that the color orange is dominating this graph. That is ok, but now you need to determine how to work around those family obligations and still achieve your professional goals. Are you noting that there is an abundance of orange, but none of it is time that you have carved out for you, personally? Be sure to "give yourself to yourself first before you give away" to your business. Include some time for you.

Do you see an abundance of green? Have you turned into a full-time volunteer for chambers and boards instead of a "showing up" in your business as a sales professional? Sometime we sit on so many committees and attend so many leads groups that we do not have time to cultivate those relationships, follow up with leads from those sources and actually SELL. Consider what meetings are the most productive for your business, and eliminate a few that no longer serve your objectives.

Adding these two colors first reveals to you why you may or may not be as productive as you want to be.

Now that you have added your first two colors, **you may want to adjust your schedule** before you complete the remainder of this exercise. You may want to rearrange your personal time. You may decide to eliminate some "regularly scheduled" meetings that are not a good use of your time. Take a moment to make those revisions now, and then move on to the next color.

"I am fired up and ready to start an awesome week tomorrow! Thanks to YOU. I am getting my old self back! Focused... driven... dedicated to making things happen. On my list (that is TIME BLOCKED, of course!!) I have a note to call you tomorrow."

A salesperson that participated in the pilot efficiency classes

GREEN – DOLLAR PRODUCING ACTIVITES

Green is the next color you need to add to your graph and represents dollar-producing activities. They are the most important activities you can build into your schedule. There are only two:

1. Making Prospecting Phone Calls ("Happy Hour")
2. Meeting Prospects

Since these activities require face to face and voice to voice interaction, we can only effectively execute them during our peak dollar producing hours. Your industry will dictate the best times of day to schedule these in.

"If it's important, do it before 11." – Gary Keller

When Gary Keller quoted these words to live by… words I refer to as a "sales commandment"… I believe he was referring to the time of day you make your most important, appointment setting phone calls. Many sales professionals are functioning inside of "I'm done" mode after lunch appointments are complete. If appointment setting calls do not get done prior to their lunch appointments, there is a good chance the calls will not happen. I understand that in some industries, phone calls may be more effective in the evening when families are home. However, in most industries, it is most effective and efficient to get those appointment setting calls completed before 11am. The bottom line: you will not have appointments if you do not make your phone calls. They need to be top priority.

Is there a conflict between when you should be prospecting and meeting with clients and when your reoccurring meetings and personal time is taking place? If so, you have pinpointed one of the obstacles holding you back from greater sales success. Do whatever you can to reschedule or eliminate the obstacles. Dirk Zeller said:

> *"To ensure you accomplish high payoff activities daily, block them into your schedule. Create a specific time slot for prospecting daily. Make a time for lead follow-up daily. Schedule them both in and be militant with keeping other low pay off activities out of those slots. Turn your cell phone and pager off during those time slots, and then you can focus with intensity on prospecting and lead follow-up."*

Easy to say, not as easy to do. But at least now you know one of the secrets of the high producers. Additional ideas:

- Block at least five hours (the more the better) in your week for **appointment setting phone calls for prospecting only**. These are not "touching base with current clients" calls. Your ONLY objective of these calls is to book your desired number of weekly PROSPECTING appointments. This is phone work only.

- Block into your graph the number of prospecting appointments you WOULD LIKE to accomplish every week. That way they are pre-scheduled into your calendar and your Time Mastery Graph.

- Block in evening and weekend prospecting appointments if your industry requires it.

- Finally, block in the number of appointments you would like to allocate to your clients. If you are in relationship selling, you will need some time every week or every two weeks to reconnect with clients over the phone or in person. I prefer to meet with my top clients over lunches or dinners a few times a month to give them my undivided attention and a substantial amount of time to convey my appreciation to them. Dinners allow me to do this without jeopardizing my most dollar producing hours for prospecting.

Time Blocking - A Sample Weekly Snapshot

8:00
8:30
9:00
9:30
10:00
10:30
11:00
11:30
12:00
12:30
1:00
1:30
2:00
2:30
3:00
3:30
4:00
4:30
5:00
5:30
6:00
6:30
7:00

Monday

Hour of Power
& Weekend Follow Up

Client Lunch or Coffee

Family Night

Tuesday

Hour of Power

Appointments:
Listing Presentations
Buyer Interviews
Coffee Appointments

Wednesday

Broker Opens &
Property Previews

Offi ce Meeting

Client Lunch or Coffee

Personal Night

Thursday

Hour of Power

Appointments:
Listing Presentations
Buyer Interviews
Coffee Appointments

Friday

8:00 Marketing Mtng.

Date Night

Need more appointments, not enough time…
Do you look at your graph and feel you need more visibility? Do you need to squeeze in a few more appointments to meet your desired quota? I have found there to be a socially accepted and almost expected rhythm to certain types of appointments. Tighten up your schedule and do some quick arranging according to these suggestions:

- Drop-by's at a prospects office can gain you visibility without a lengthy appointment, running about 15 minutes. Bring something of value to "get in and get out."

- In-office consultative appointments can run as short as 30 to 45 minutes if you accomplish them efficiently. They are quick to plan and convenient for the client/prospective client.

- Coffee appointments tend to run 45 to 60 minutes. Coffee appointments are perfect for qualifying candidates for your prospecting efforts. There is ease of access, and they allow for a low investment of time and cost. Coffee appointments are great for meeting people to whom you were just referred. They are also great for second meetings to get your prospect solidly qualified as someone you want to work with.

> *"I wanted to let you know that I did my 2 hours of phone calls and you're right! I feel like a new person."*
>
> A salesperson that participated in the pilot efficiency classes

- Breakfasts run about an hour. These are great for your busy prospects who are "rise and shiners" and do not have time to "mess around."

- Lunches can be lengthy, running about 60 to 90 minutes. Save these for client appreciation meetings or for your top prospects. They are more of a dollar and time investment, so do not waste them on anyone who you are not currently working with or who is not a top qualified prospect. Only give your time and money away to people who deserve it.

- Dinners are the most time and money consuming, generally running two hours or more. These are most appropriate for client appreciation meetings or cream of the crop prospects. Again, only give your time and money away to people who deserve it.

- Put together "coffee hours" and "cocktail hours" and invite both clients and prospects to attend. If you offer to pay for the appetizers, or for the coffee and danishes, your expense stays relatively low considering the number of people who may attend. You can leverage your time with minimum expense and still get some great visibility.

PURPLE – PROJECTS AND PLANNING
Next, you will add in purple. Purple represents that block of time that is easily overlooked and forgotten when you start proactively prioritizing your time. Yet, many sales people find it to be one of the MAIN THINGS that sweeps them along the path of poor time management and derails them the most frequently.

Time Blocking - A Sample Weekly Snapshot

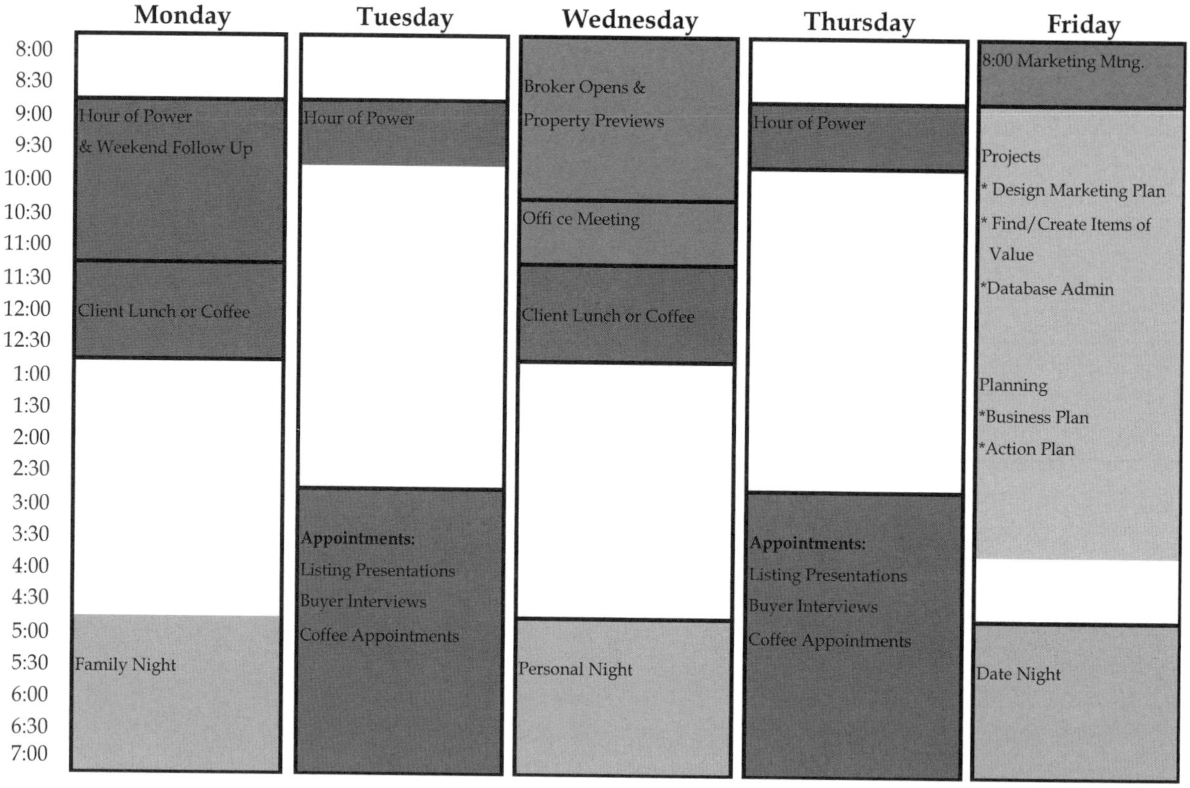

	Monday	Tuesday	Wednesday	Thursday	Friday
8:00					8:00 Marketing Mtng.
8:30			Broker Opens &		
9:00	Hour of Power	Hour of Power	Property Previews	Hour of Power	
9:30	& Weekend Follow Up				Projects
10:00					* Design Marketing Plan
10:30			Offi ce Meeting		* Find/Create Items of
11:00					Value
11:30					*Database Admin
12:00	Client Lunch or Coffee		Client Lunch or Coffee		
12:30					
1:00					Planning
1:30					*Business Plan
2:00					*Action Plan
2:30					
3:00					
3:30		**Appointments:**		**Appointments:**	
4:00		Listing Presentations		Listing Presentations	
4:30		Buyer Interviews		Buyer Interviews	
5:00		Coffee Appointments		Coffee Appointments	
5:30	Family Night		Personal Night		Date Night
6:00					
6:30					
7:00					

It is easy to get lost inside of projects and planning for two main reasons.

1. Projects can be creative and therefore fun. Finding interesting information such as websites or articles to pass along to your clients, building blogs, and working on social media sites are all very interesting. And while it is fun, it can also be, unfortunately, distracting.

2. Projects can also be very taxing, becoming something that we have to push ourselves through. If you have been putting something off for a long time, it will eventually demand your attention. Cleaning up your email, handling months of accounting gone awry and overhauling your database are examples.

Yes, projects and planning are important and just **do not** do them during your dollar productive time slots. Promise? Here are my suggestions:

- To be highly effective, you must set up tomorrow before it arrives. Schedule ten minutes at the end of every workday for planning the next day. Make a list of tasks to complete. From that list, select your top three that you MUST execute. Decide when to do them. This habit alone will make an incredible shift in your efficiency. Every one minute of planning time will save about ten minutes of work.

- Schedule time weekly for accomplishing small projects and weekly planning. (Currently, I schedule about 5 hours a week for this). If you have this time already pre-planned into your schedule, it will be easier to give yourself permission to postpone a project until that allotted time arrives. It gives you a mental cushion of comfort to know that you do not have to worry about "getting to something". Sometimes giving yourself permission to NOT to do something can be just as important as giving yourself permission TO DO something.

- Schedule some time every month to work on larger projects. (Personally, I schedule in two four-hour time blocks over the weekends to accomplish this). If you have a presentation you need to put together, presentation folders to prepare, or need substantial time to work on your database and email folders, this extended project and planning time is the time block in which to accomplish that.

YELLOW – ADMINISTRATIVE TASKS

Finally, we add in the color yellow. YELLOW represents the time we use to execute our administrative tasks and current transaction-driven tasks.

- Schedule in some time every morning for "**Daily Prep.**" These tasks can be accomplished in thirty minutes or less per day. This is the time you check email and voice mail that trickled in while you slept and return the "A" priority calls and emails. Quickly review today's task list you established the night before and today's calendar.

- Schedule some time to make proactive phone calls to **clients in transaction** with you. We generally get bombarded with client driven calls and tasks all throughout the day. If you proactively launch a preemptive strike every day to make these kinds of calls, you will lessen the number of calls coming into you.

- Schedule time every day to **handle final follow up**. I call this time, "Completions and Deliverables." Give it an hour or two every day. Most frequently, this is useful to do at the end of the day after you have attended appointments and now have deliverables to send out to your clients. Follow up from the momentum you have created that day. Tie up loose ends and finish the day feeling like you have accomplished everything you needed to - that you "finished what you started." What a great feeling! There is nothing worse than coming to work the next day only to discover that you have five things to do from the day before that now MUST get done… and at that point it will probably interfere with your time to place prospecting phone calls and appointment setting. Completions and Deliverables can happen anytime at the end of the day, either 3pm or midnight, whatever works for your schedule, family and industry.

> *"I've been finding huge benefit in Efficiency by Design. For example, the time blocking is helping to keep me focused on what is important and when. The concept of separating out the Dollar Productive tasks, administration and projects and planning are making a difference. The task tracker and hot sheet are going to be great too."*
>
> A salesperson that participated in the pilot efficiency classes

- Schedule time every quarter for an organizational day. I refer to this as a "**Super Saturday.**" The Super Saturday is your key organizational day. Clean out files, both paper and digital. Organize your computer desktop. Read the materials that have piled up over time such as magazines, periodicals and archive items into file folders. Remove or refine your systems. Again, if you have this time already pre-planned in your schedule, it will be much easier to give yourself permission to NOT work on time-costly tasks and projects until your organizational day arrives.

Time Blocking - A Sample Weekly Snapshot

	Monday	Tuesday	Wednesday	Thursday	Friday
8:00	"Daily Disciplines"	"Daily Disciplines"		"Daily Disciplines"	8:00 Marketing Mtng.
8:30			Broker Opens &		
9:00	Hour of Power	Hour of Power	Property Previews	Hour of Power	
9:30	& Weekend Follow Up				Projects
10:00					* Design Marketing Plan
10:30			Offi ce Meeting		* Find/Create Items of
11:00		Current Client Files &		Current Client Files &	Value
11:30		Buyer Previews		Buyer Previews	*Database Admin
12:00	Client Lunch or Coffee		Client Lunch or Coffee		
12:30					
1:00					Planning
1:30	Current Client Files &		Current Client Files &		*Business Plan
2:00	Buyer Previews	Completions	Buyer Previews	Completions	*Action Plan
2:30					
3:00					
3:30		**Appointments:**		**Appointments:**	
4:00	Completions	Listing Presentations	Completions	Listing Presentations	Completions
4:30		Buyer Interviews		Buyer Interviews	
5:00		Coffee Appointments		Coffee Appointments	
5:30	Family Night		Personal Night		Date Night
6:00					
6:30					
7:00					

COMPLETING YOUR FINAL DRAFT

Now that you have added your five time blocking elements into your graph using color, you can more easily see how to efficiently use your time on a daily, weekly and monthly basis. You can see more clearly how much you can accomplish.

I suggest you now go back online to www.EfficiencyByDesignOnline.com and download the Excel spreadsheet for this graph. Save it to your computer, and use Excel's coloring tool to fill in this graph. Once it is complete, you can reference this tool to pre-build your calendar and begin implementing Time Mastery into every day.

D. Implementation

We need to move you from having been interested to taking action. Make the commitment to improve your business.

My Commitment to My Business

- I will TAKE ACTION to make a difference in my business, TODAY!
- I stay CORE (Centered on Results Every Day).
- I EXECUTE what I am learning. I am not a perpetual student.

My greatest "AHA!" moments from this chapter were:

My 24 hour Commitment is (what idea related to this chapter can I implement in 24 hours):

My Seven Day Commitment is:

My new standard of professional excellence or habitual way of working is:

What does Success Look Like?

It is important to note that if you are doing the majority of the things suggested the majority of the time, THAT IS SUCCESS. It is not possible to do all things, all of the time. However, if you can honestly look at yourself and say you are doing what you need to be doing about 51% of the time, its time to give yourself a pat on the back. You are doing great!

What is in the next chapter?

Do you feel like you have handle on Time Mastery? Now you need the tools to execute your time mastery plan. A great next step can be discovered is in Chapter 7… Piles to Files. You will learn how to tame the email monster, get your paper files well organized, and develop an operations manual. I would recommend investing some time on Chapter 7 if your report card scored a B or below on that segment.

7. From Piles to Files:

Essential Systems, Tips and Tools to GET ORGANIZED

A place for everything, everything in its place.
Benjamin Franklin

How Does "Piles to Files" Fit Into the System?
There are four Cornerstones of success. You do not necessarily need to master each of them to move on to the more advanced concepts. However, before moving on, you should be able to answer at least "neutral" instead of "disagree" on most of the Cornerstone questions on the survey in the beginning of the book.

This chapter will help you understand:

1. The Paper Filing System
2. The Email Filing System
3. The Operations Manual
4. Implementation

When you finish "Piles to Files," you will progress to "Daily Disciplines," which builds on your skills.

Introduction
Over the number of years that I have coached sales professionals, one concept has always surfaced as a "truth." It is difficult to focus on establishing new working habits when your "old ways" of doing things are lurking around you. If you want to sell more, you need to clean up your act. Literally. This includes cleaning up your office and the environments in which you spend most of your mental and physical time. This chapter will help you accomplish that with simple systems that are easy to incorporate and have a powerful effect in getting you organized.

The systems you will CONCEPTUALLY learn in this chapter can be easily applied in your other environments to create new order and organization in your business, resulting in new sales.

Proof that filing systems are an essential component of your success is in the survey box:

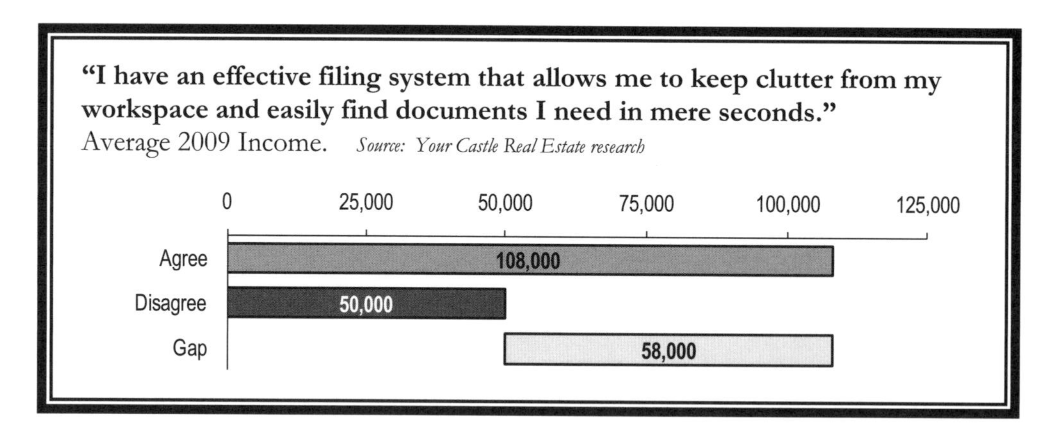

We asked sales people on the survey, "What challenges do you face with filing and organization?"

- "I have systems in place, but I can easily get off track to respond to something with an immediate need. Filing system is a constant challenge. It is a challenge keeping track of who got what and what is next." (Income over $100K)
- "I am a packrat. I am sometimes overwhelmed with unsorted papers."
- "Sometimes creating a system or learning the use of a new tool seems to require too much time."

We asked on the survey, "What is working well for you?"

- "I delegate everything to assistants." (Income over $100K)

Yes, delegation probably is the BEST answer and my overall goal is to help you become so productive that you can afford to acquire assistance, if you choose. This may not be a realistic solution for you right now. Even if you were able to hire an assistant tomorrow, you would still need to establish certain systems first, before delegation can occur. Alternatively, you would need to develop systems along side of your assistant so they could adequately understand your business and properly support you. Either way, you still need to play a proactive role in establishing systems for your business, even if someone else is implementing them. You might as well begin the journey.

In this chapter, I am going to introduce you to three simple filing systems needed by sales professionals:

1. Paper Filing System
2. Email Filing System
3. Operations Manual

Let's walk through each of these systems.

1. Paper Filing System

Your paper filing system will consist of three elements:

A. The Working File Drawer
B. Client & Prospect Files
C. Archives

This table summarizes some of the key characteristics of the elements.

	The Working File Drawer	Client & Prospect Files	Archives
Urgency	Immediate In-Process	Immediate In-Process	Not Immediate Not in process
Suggested placement in your office	Close to your chair. Opposite of your writing hand when possible. Not visible	To the side of or behind your desk, such as on a book shelf or Credenza. Visible	Behind your desk or in a separate room altogether. Not visible
Inclusions – What files do you store or include in each of these systems?	Priorities A-C Projects 1-5 Administrative Forms Expense Records and Receipts Database Maintenance Upcoming Meeting Notes and Agendas Events Invitations and Driving Directions	Open client files. Current Prospect Files	Resources Tools Reference Materials Vendor Information Presentation Kits Closed Client Files
Color of file folders	Based on Time Blocking	Yellow	Black or Olive

A: The Working File Drawer

Don't agonize, organize.
Florynce Kennedy

Even though so many of us are paper "less" or even paper free, there is still a need for paper in our lives. We need to have a simple, easy system to accommodate storage and use of those documents so they do not overwhelm our desk… or our office floor. The Working File Drawer is my solution to your paper problem.

This drawer should be located IN your desk, in a file drawer on the opposite side of your writing hand when possible. You need easy and immediate access to this drawer daily, because of the nature of the documents you will be storing in it. It is not intended to store much – so it can be small.

> *"I purchased some colored files and started my work drawer; I have to admit I really feel much better having an actual system in place. Before, I was just piling (and hiding) instead of filing. Hopefully, I will actually use the system, and not just have my piles in drawers, but I feel really confident that won't happen. I may have to take a peek at your book again, so I can set one up for myself. I wanted to thank you for, well, everything."*
>
> A salesperson that participated in the pilot efficiency classes

The Fear Factor (Fear of Filing)
Before I get further into the idea of the "Working File Drawer," I need to address what 99 percent of you are thinking: "*Darice, I want a clean desk, but I don't want to file anything. If it's not in front of me, I may forget about it!*"

Yes… I know this concept of filing might seem overwhelming at first. Yes… you will need to change a habit. Just remember that the function of your Working File Drawer is very simple. It is simply taking your "pile of now" (all the papers currently on your desk and in your briefcase) and transforming it into "folders of WOW!" It is literally taking horizontal piles and turning them into vertical files.

Here are two GREAT things about this system:

1. Once you get your Working File Drawer set up and prioritize your "pile of now" documents into files, you will immediately experience an energy shift. Your mindset will change from feeling overwhelmed to feeling that the tasks of the day are manageable. You have to trust me on this. Try it. It is the only way you will understand how this works.

2. You will begin to find items quickly and never lose track of anything. The TRICK is using your drawer the same way you would use your desk. **The key is to use it. Work from this drawer.** Stay aware of the contents of this drawer every day. This is where the shift in thought and habit comes in.

Setting up Your Working File Drawer
You will need the following supplies to set up your Working File Drawer:

- Colored Hanging Folders
- Plastic Tabs
- Post-It Notes
- Manila Folders

The colors of your hanging folders will reflect the colors you applied to use in your time blocking system (Chapter 6 – Time Mastery). Here is a recap of the colors and their meanings:

Folder Color	Associated Action or Activity
Green	Dollar Producing Activities
Yellow	Administrative Tasks
Purple	Projects and Planning
Blue	Meetings (Non-Dollar Productive)
Orange	Personal
Red	ACTION ITEMS

About the Color Red
The color we add to your efficiency system at this point is red. We use red to signify ACTION. In your Working File Drawer, you will create three action folders that you will label A, B and C. You will use these red folders daily. You will prioritize documents that require action into these three folders using the following prioritization strategy:

Label	Contents	Color
A	**ABSOLUTELY** must be done today	Red
B	Do **BEFORE** week-end	Red
C	**COULD** be done before month-end	Red

Here is the behavioral change that will make you more successful: Create the habit of looking through your three red folders at the beginning and the end of every day. Process the papers within your "A" folder daily. Then, move papers through your red action folders at the end of every day. For example:

- Papers inside of the B Priority folder will become A Priorities at some point during the week.
- Anything moved from the B folder to the A folder means it is has become an A priority for tomorrow.
- C Priority papers may eventually move to the B Priority folder.
- It is not uncommon for many C Priority papers to eventually get tossed into the trash and never even make it into the A and B folders. The C folder frequently holds things we THINK we want to work on, but in the end turn out to be unimportant, after all. I will generally clean out my C folder during a weekly admin time block or a Super Saturday.

Labeling Your "Other" Folders in your Working File Drawer
From my coaching experience, I have noticed a great deal of similarities in how sales professionals set up their Working File Drawer. Here is a list of the most commonly used labels for your folders. Of course, you may come up with more labels, or completely different labels altogether, but this list will help you conceptualize this tool and get you started:

Folder Label	Folder Contents	Folder Color
Project 1 **Project 2** **Project 3** **Project 4** **Project 5**	These hanging folders act as catch-all, rotating folders for marketing initiatives, marketing content ideas, marketing samples, business partnering ideas, strategic business planning, etc.	Purple
Forms	Store blank Efficiency by Design forms you use frequently such Call Logs, Daily Planning Pages and other CORE Forms	Yellow
Expenses	Use as a catch-all for receipts, expense reports, etc.	Yellow
Database Maintenance	Use as a catch-all for database changes and additions including returned mail, office rosters, etc.	Yellow
To Review/Read	Use as a catch-all for publications, articles, etc. This folder can get very large very fast, so be sure to schedule time into your month to make your way through this folder and clean it out frequently	Yellow
Events	Use as a place to store invitations, driving directions, and other information **on events you are attending**. For events you are **planning**, use the purple "project" folders.	Green
Meetings	Use as a catch all for agenda item ideas, notes you are jotting down to prepare for a meeting, etc. Remember, these are not meetings you have with your prospects. Instead, they are non-dollar producing meetings such as board meetings, team meetings, sales meetings, etc.	Blue
Personal	Personal items	Orange

Getting Your PILES into FILES (How to Organize Your Working File Drawer)
After setting up your Working File Drawer with your colored folders, the process of getting your piles into files is simple. To begin, I suggest you gather all of your "piles" that are in your immediate workspace, such as your desk and your briefcase, and put them together into only one pile. Then, take a deep breath and begin the process of getting that pile into your Working File Drawer." With each piece of paper, ask yourself:

What is this piece of paper? What is my next step with it?

Many of your piles will likely be filed into the A, B, and C action items folders. Some will be filed into other working drawer folders. Some will not be appropriate for the working file drawer, and will need to be archived. You will immediately find that once you have completed filing your original "pile of NOW" into your Working File Drawer, it will be very easy to maintain your system. From this point forward, quickly process any new papers that cross your desk or end up your briefcase by doing on of the following:

- Scan and store it digitally.
- Read it and discard it.
- File it appropriately into your working files or archives.

If it DOES require action, it would go into one of your three ACTION files (A, B or C). If it DOES NOT require action but you need to hang onto it, you will be filing it away into one of your other folders. Depending upon the nature of the document, it will either end up in a folder within your Working File Drawer, or it will be archived.

This is a simple tool! Enjoying its benefits boils down to two things: DISCIPLINE and INTENTION. If you have a high intention to get organized and stay organized and the discipline to consistently work your processes, keeping this system intact is not only easy… it will change the way you process your papers, forever. It also supports your new mindset about how you use your time as it relates to processing paperwork.

Additional Filing Components:
I have explained in detail what DOES go into your Working File Drawer. It is equally important to explain what DOES NOT go into your Working File Drawer. That is where the two other components of your paper filing system come into play: Client and Prospect Files and Archives.

B: Client and Prospect Files

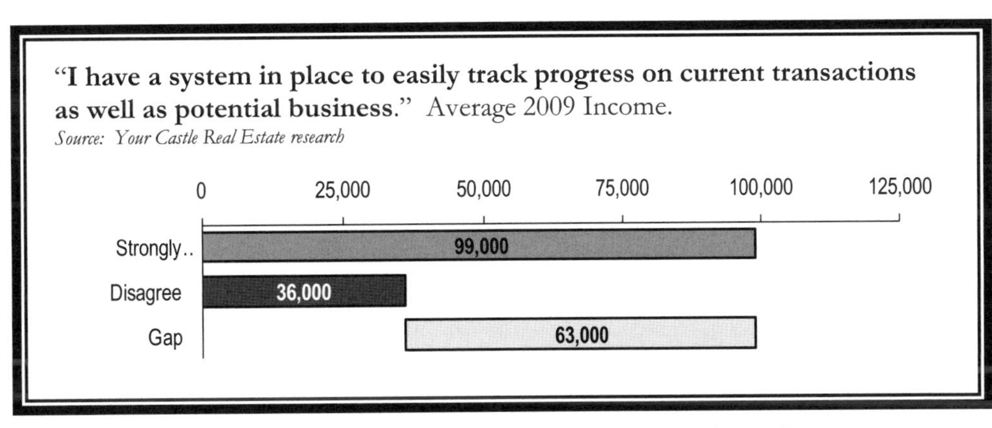

These refer to your files on current transactions (with clients) as well as files you have started compiling during the course of your prospecting efforts. Location of these files is important. These files should NOT be stored on your desk. Instead, place them to the left or right of your desk, either in drawers or on a credenza for easy access. Pull them onto your desk when working with them, and the replace them when you are done. I also suggest using a process checklist. This checklist should be inserted into each of your folders and used throughout the course of the transaction. This checklist ensures that you, or your assistant, do not miss any pertinent dates, deadlines or deliverables.

Does this really matter? Look at the survey results!

Based on the income difference, I would say YES, filing systems and process checklists for client and prospecting files really do matter.

C: Archives

It is important to differentiate between "working" files versus "archived" files. Remember, the Working File Drawer is "your pile of NOW." It holds documents that pertain to your current action items or items that you use or reference frequently. Archived files, on the other hand, hold documents that you reference very infrequently or hold materials needed for presentation purposes. Typical items you archive might include:

- Reference materials
- Vendor information
- Resources and tools
- Taxes, accounting receipts
- Closed client files
- Marketing materials for presentation packets
- Complete presentation packets that are "ready to go"
- Keepsake items such as cards, letters and testimonials
- "How-to Guides" including operation manuals for hardware or electronics

> *"For my business, the 'Time Management' and 'Piles to Files' workshops provided the largest benefit.*
>
> *By looking at my past schedules, I determined how reactive to e-mails and the telephone that I had become and how that was preventing the implementation of more effective projects. By scheduling key activities ahead of time and turning off the phone and e-mail, I am getting projects completed that have even greater benefit for my clients. I am also finding that many of the little fires seem to extinguish themselves."*
>
> A salesperson that participated in the pilot efficiency classes

The placement of your archived files is very important. These files should never distract you or be visible. They should be concealed in filing cabinets which are located either behind you when as you are sitting at your desk, or in a separate room altogether. I suggest using either black or olive colored folders to distinguish that these folders are "inactive."

The Proof is in…The Pictures

My experience with top producers is that many (not all) are well-organized people. Those top producers who are NOT well-organized but succeed IN SPITE of their organizational dysfunctionalities could either be making more money; working fewer hours, *or both* if they did improve this element of their business.

Another frequent finding of mine is the top producer who finally recognizes their lack of organization and acknowledges their need for assistance. These top producers will hire an assistant who has an organizational edge. This strategic move gives the top producer the organizational support they need while opening up their schedule to stay focused on what they do best: sell.

Most of us have been resisting organization since we were kids when our mother first started "encouraging" us to clean up our rooms. My friends, it is time to acknowledge Mom for her infinite wisdom…and START GETTING ORGANIZED!

Be Inspired!
Creating order and organization in your filing systems moves you from this… to this.

Before

After

Or from this… to this.

Before

After

These are the offices of two of my actual clients, before and after they implemented the Efficiency by Design paper filing system.

2. The Email Filing System

One of the advantages of being disorderly is that one is constantly making exciting discoveries.
A. A. Milne

Interestingly, our survey findings with technology and organization were consistent with our other organizational findings.

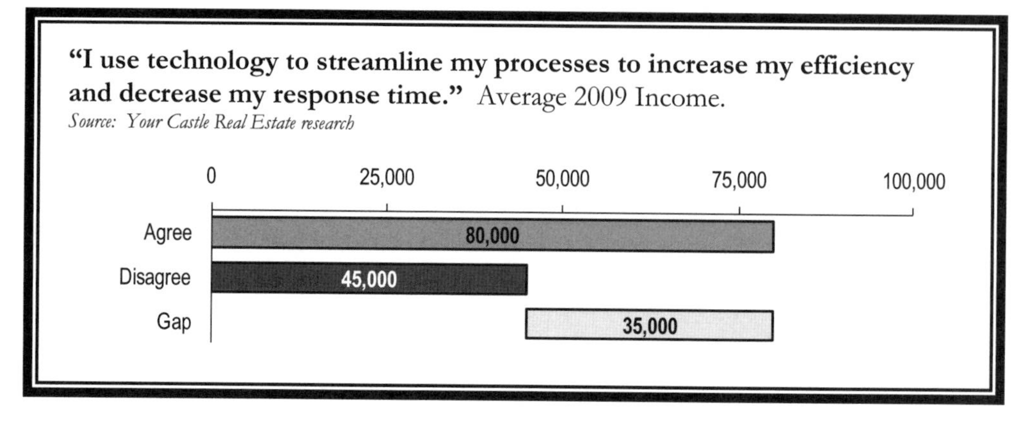

We asked people what challenges they faced with technology and efficiency. Here were some of their thoughts:

- "One program does not offer everything. I would like a program to have an e-mail drip campaign, contact management, finance/budgeting, advertising, etc. It would be cool to have everything under one umbrella."
- "I am not very tech-savvy and sometimes the new technology scares me because I just do not get it."
- "I know how, but I lack the discipline to do it."
- "I am getting so busy that I do not make the time to implement the systems and record keeping."
- "I would also like to be able to organize my contacts based on their wish list so I can more easily follow up with them."

What is working well for you for managing email?

- "I set up an email folder for every transaction. Then when I respond to an email, it is filed automatically. That way, the only the emails in my inbox need to be managed. I also carbon myself on all of the important emails, then I will never have someone say they did not receive it, nor mince my words. This has saved me several times. I always have documents for lots of previous transactions that I can pull in seconds." (Income over $100K)

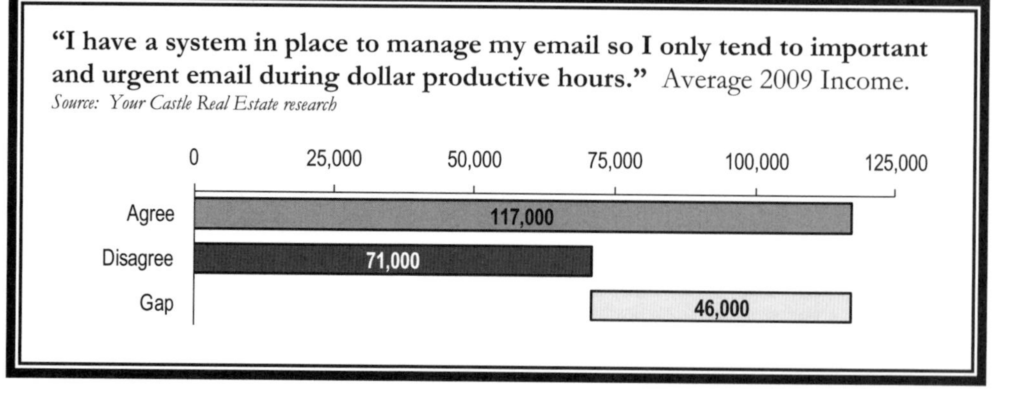

- "Having sub files on my email that I can file items in, rather than print them, allows me to be more organized and efficient."

Taming the Email Giant
Our email filing systems looks strikingly similar to our paper filing system. I use the same ideas and the same colors to help you keep the flow of the filing concept together.

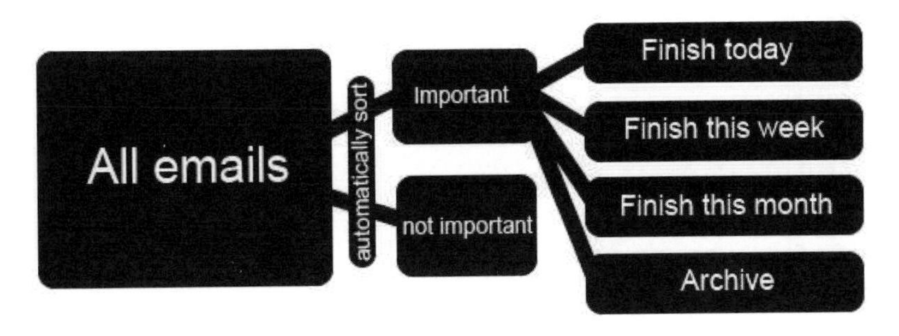

Above is a diagram of my suggested email flow. The appendix of this book will walk you step-by-step to launch this system into your email program using Outlook as the example. Here are some KEY IDEAS on how to best use your email system:

The Email Inbox

- Your email *inbox* should contain emails that require **immediate communication ONLY**. Keep only those items that need communication in your inbox, and flag them as RED if your email system has a flag function.
- Move any emails out of your inbox that do not require attention NOW but do need your attention later. File these emails into the user-defined folders, usually located to the left of the inbox. Label the folders in a way that correspond with the time blocking we covered in the earlier chapter. Most email systems have an active inbox *and* user-created folders. Learn how to use your user-created folders, as that will be an essential part in "taming your email giant."
- Open these user-defined folders during your specified time block and begin addressing these emails. See the screen shot below to get a visual of this process.

Sorting your inbox and moving your email into user-defined folders is the same process as taking your "pile of NOW" and sorting it into the vertical files in your working file drawer. To begin the sorting and filing process, I suggest first collapsing the groups within your email inbox and only viewing those emails that pertain to "today." Then move onto yesterday, last week, and so on. This allows you to concentrate on one day at a time to get these emails filed, instead of being reminded of all the things you "should have done" in the past.

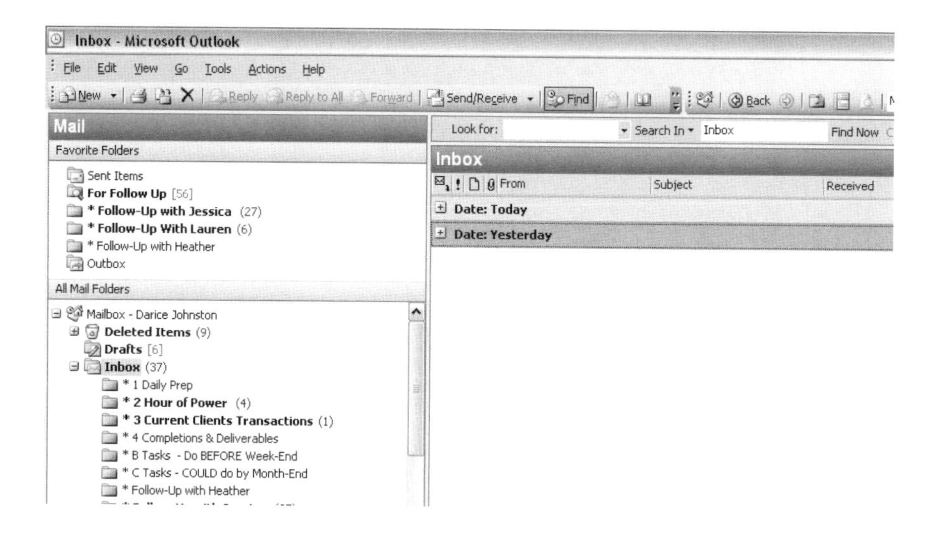

Your Email Archives

- Use your email archives in the exact same way you use your paper file archives.
- This folder, or folders, should act as a point of reference for you. Store information such as:
    - Newsletters that you would like to read later
    - Reference materials
    - Vendor information
    - Resources and tools
    - Keepsake items

- You can have archive-able material sent directly into your archive folders by utilizing the "Rules" feature in your email program. By adding a rule, you can require emails received by a particular sender to bypass your inbox altogether and get stored directly into the archived folder of your choice. This allows you to control your level of distractions during the workday and stay focused on work-related emails… instead of being visually distracted and ultimately derailed by items of personal interest as they filter in. See the appendix for step-by-step directions.

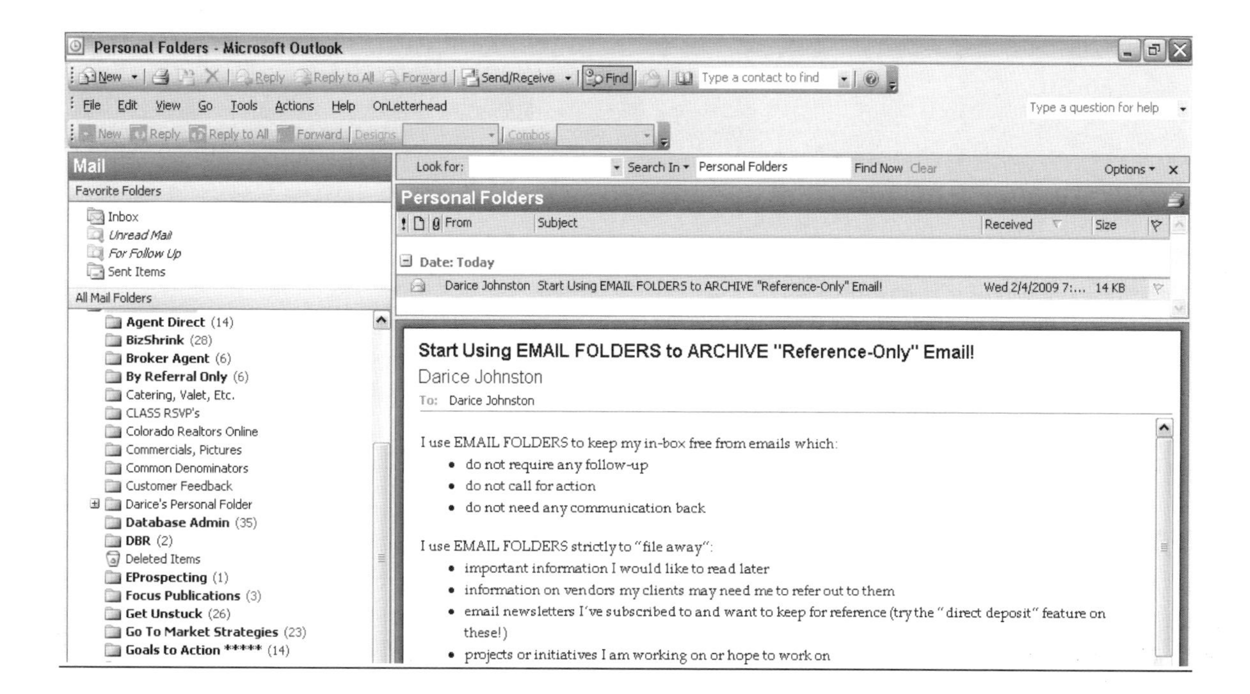

3. The Operations Manual

Early in my career, I felt that organization would destroy my creativity. Now, I feel the opposite. Discipline is the concrete that allows you to be creative.
Verna Gibson

As paperless as I try to be, my love for the art of penmanship is still very strong. I love to hold a pen in my hand and write. I also admit that I like to see certain documents in front of me, as opposed to looking at them on a computer screen or my Blackberry. For this reason I have established a tool that I refer to as my Operations Manual. This professional looking and well-organized three-ring binder allows me to carry my most frequently referenced information and the forms I use to execute my day-to-day processes.

What your Operations Manual **IS designed to hold:**

- Your most frequently referenced information.
- Your most-needed daily/weekly/monthly organizational tools.
- Your prospecting system by which to execute your dollar-producing activities.

What Your Operations Manual **IS NOT designed to hold:**

- Piles of disorganized, loose papers.
- If you are carrying around a stack of loose papers, this is a clue that you are not utilizing your Working File Drawer correctly.

Your Operations Manual **should be:**

- Attractive and functional – I suggest a ½ inch, 8 1/2 x 11 leather, 3-ring binder.
- Portable – it should be easy to pack up into your briefcase.

- Accessible – it should be kept open on your desk or other space where you most often find yourself working.

The Components of Your Operations Manual

- Index page – you will type page then laminate it or slide it into a plastic sheet cover
- 5 tab dividers
- Clear business card sleeves
- 3-ring compatible pocket folders
- Plastic sheet covers
- Lined notepad or thin notebook
- Daily planning pages, prospecting pages and other forms. Items marked with an asterisk* below are forms available for downloading and customizing at www.EfficiencyByDesignOnline.com

Suggested tabs and content ideas for your Operations Manual:

Tab	Labels	Content
1	CORE documents	• Daily Planning Pages* • CORE Weekly Action Plan* • Quarterly and Annual Plan* • Colored Time Mastery Graph* • Mock Monthly Calendar for standing appointments and standing deadlines • Incoming Call Log*
2	Power Partners, Service Providers & Resources	• Business cards of your partners • Your company roster • Key reference information on service providers / concierge list
3	Projects & Planning	• Weekly Planning Page* • The Portable Project Board * • The Parking Lot* • Planning pages for individual projects • Marketing campaign planning pages*
4	Personal	• Gratitude Journal • Financial Information • Daily Health Journal
5	Hour of Power	• The Hot Sheet* • Business Cards of "Just Mets" • Pocket folder to act as a catch-all for items such as "napkin notes" • Sales Tracks Planning Page *(see Chapter on Mastering The Art of Follow-Up)
	Also Carry	• Note cards, Stamps, Business Cards • Pocket folder for your "A" Action File Papers

Think it through… for YOU

We have touched on the idea of cleaning up your office environment using the three tools suggested in this chapter. However, in today's age of technology, you can no longer consider your office to be the only work environment. Many sales professionals have two physical offices – one at home and one within their company. In addition, laptops, BlackBerries and iPhones create virtual offices anywhere. These items are just as essential a component to the organization and functionality of your business as your physical office. Here is a list of common work "environments":

1. Desk (home and away)
2. Computer (desktop/shortcuts/folders)
3. Email Box (inbox/folders)
4. Internet Browser (favorites/internet feeds)
5. Filing Cabinets (folders)
6. Cell Phone (sync/functionality/ease of use)
7. Car
8. Planner/Daytimer
9. Purse and Briefcase

Make a list of all of the "places" where you work and all of the "environments" you work within:

____________________________ ____________________________

____________________________ ____________________________

____________________________ ____________________________

The bottom line? Wherever you are… THAT is your office! To increase your sales effectiveness, make sure your environments are organized, functional and allow you to work efficiently every day.

4. Implementation

We need to move you from having been interested to taking action. Make the commitment to improve your business.

My Commitment to My Business

- I will TAKE ACTION to make a difference in my business, TODAY!
- I stay CORE (Centered on Results Every Day).
- I EXECUTE what I am learning. I am not a perpetual student.

My greatest "AHA!" moments from this chapter were:

____

____

____

My 24 hour Commitment is (what idea related to this chapter can I implement in 24 hours):

____

____

____

____

My Seven Day Commitment is:

____

____

____

____

My new standard of professional excellence or habitual way of working is:

____

____

____

What does Success look like?
It is important to note that if you are doing **the majority** of the things suggested in this chapter **the majority** of the time, THAT IS SUCCESS. It is not possible to do all things, all of the time. However, if you can honestly look at yourself and say that you are doing what you need to be doing about 51% of the time, that is success.

What is in the next chapter?
Do you feel like you have a handle on Piles to Files? The next secret of highly efficient sales professionals is revealed in Chapter 8, "Daily Disciplines." Recall from the introduction pages of this book that CORE stands for "Center on Results Everyday." In the next chapter you will develop a CORE weekly action plan, learn about "the parking lot" where you park great ideas that pop up during the day, learn tips for your appointment calendar and more. I would recommend investing some time on this next chapter if you scored a B or below on Daily Disciplines.

8. Establishing Strong Daily Disciplines

Discipline brings excellence, and excellence brings freedom.
Dan Milman (Writer, Speaker, Olympic Gymnast)

How Do the "Daily Disciplines" Fit Into the System?
There are four Cornerstones of success. You do not necessarily need to master each of them to move on to the more advanced concepts. However, before moving on, you should be able to answer at least "neutral" instead of "disagree" on most of the Cornerstone questions on the survey in the beginning of the book.

This chapter will help you understand the:

A. CORE Weekly Action Plan
B. The Parking Lot
C. Daily Planning Pages
D. The Appointment Calendar
E. Implementation

When you finish with "Daily Disciplines," you will progress to "Falling in Love with Your Database," which builds on your skills.

Introduction
We completed a research project for our prior book *Thrive – How Realtors Can Succeed in a Down Market.* In the survey for that project, one of the statements was, "I am effective at prioritizing my work." The sales professionals who disagreed had an average income of $76,000. Those who strongly agreed had an income of $129,000. This made us aware of the earning impact of properly prioritizing.

Prioritizing demands some degree of planning. Executing those priorities requires effective efficiency tools. In the survey utilized for UNLOCKED, our goal was to identify the key habits and disciplines that made the greatest difference in sales success. We wanted to understand the best practices of top producing sales professionals. More importantly, we wanted to provide specific advice and offer solutions to the sales professionals who wanted to improve their income while increasing the time they spent with their families. Our survey participants illuminated beautifully the relationship between planning, efficiency and income. We obtained some striking statistics to share with you.

The main objectives for this chapter are to help you:

- Get clear about your daily, weekly and monthly commitments and priorities.
- Create efficiency systems to execute those commitments.
- Expand your capacity to obtain new business.

You will accomplish this by looking differently at how you organize your daily, weekly and monthly priorities, and the habitual ways by which you work and think.

Why We Need to Plan and Prioritize on a Daily Basis
Our survey found pre-planning the day's activities to be **one of the most powerful predictors of success. The income difference is staggering:**

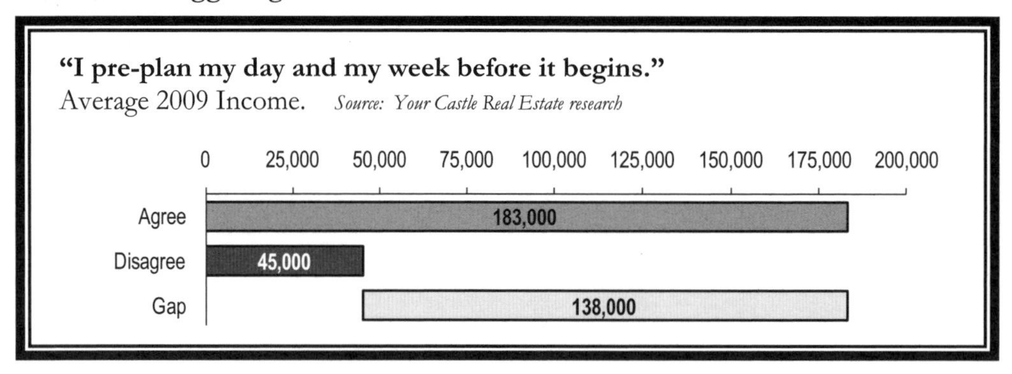

Here were some of the comments we received for the question, "What is working well for you?"

- "I have started not opening email until late in the afternoon. That got me off track."
- "Plan in the morning and be realistic with what the priorities of the day are."
- "I have a white board that I can easily write down tasks."
- "I write everything down and check off as I complete. It keeps me on task."

Here were some of the comments we received for, "What challenges do you face?"

- "Being flexible enough in my schedule to attend to a last minute crisis that comes up is challenging." (Income over $100K)
- "Every day is full of interruptions. This necessitates some elements of reactionary tasks. Closings, appraisals and lenders are just some of the many daily interruptions. Interruptions are indicators that we are fairly busy." (Income over $100K)
- "Constant fire fighting and interruptions from business partners."
- "Interruptions; I can get sidetracked with high maintenance clients."
- "Dealing with interruptions in my business... but with potential clients that I do not feel I can ignore."

We asked another question that tied to the concept of Daily Disciplines.

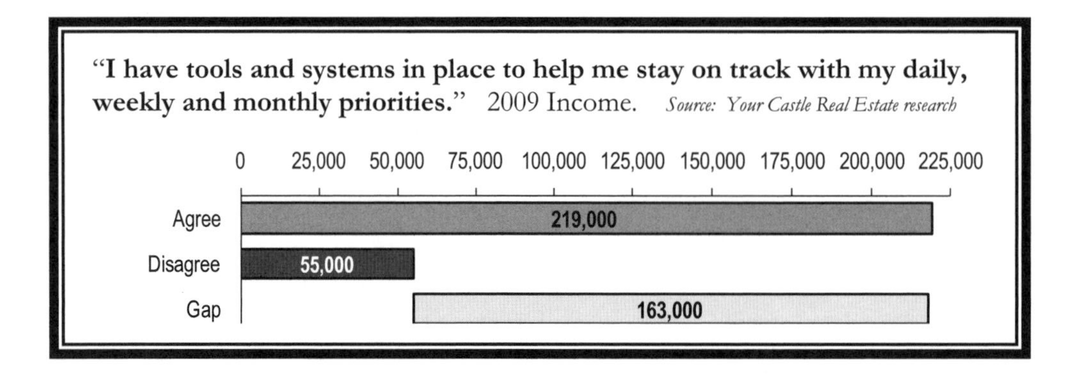

Another entirely astonishing find.

I think the message is clear: If you are willing to take the time to set up systems for planning and execution… and live by the new habits and disciplines required to work those systems… you will experience a dramatic shift in income. **If you are truly ready to make that commitment, the tools presented in this chapter will support you to make it happen.**

THE DAILY DISCIPLINE TOOLS

I created four tools for a sales professional to implement into their day-to-day processes. These will assist you in developing and sustaining new ways of working. They also support you in maintaining the consistent discipline required to attain success:

A. The CORE Weekly Action Plan
B. The Parking Lot
C. The Daily Planning Pages
D. The Appointment Calendar

We will go through each of these tools in detail.

A: The CORE Weekly Action Plan

If you want to make good use of your time, you've got to know what's most important and then give it all you've got.
Lee Iacocca

You Can Get Everything Done That NEEDS to Get Done

This is not a pipedream. It is a reality. As discussed in an earlier chapter, CORE stands for "Center on Results Every Day." Working your business and "staying CORE" is the key. Here is an illustration of how to stay focused on what matters in your business *at the time that it matters*. This visual will help you conceptually understand how to plan and prioritize your day.

> *"I sit down every night to outline the tasks that must be done the following day (pre plan). This clears my head at the end of the day and I can start fresh and quickly the next morning."*
>
> Quote from survey

Picture in your mind that you are holding a sealed mason jar filled to the brim with walnuts and rice. The walnuts represent the **key activities** that you must do every day to move your business forward. The rice represents all of the little **ancillary tasks** that you engage in that seem important or urgent, but really are not. The rice also represents the distractions that take you away from the most important, dollar productive activities of your day-to-day business.

If I were to ask you to open the jar, empty the contents and then reload the contents, your process in accomplishing this would be very revealing. If you begin haphazardly sweeping the contents back into the jar, it will not all fit properly. You will not be able to get all of the walnuts OR all of the rice back into the jar. If you put a portion of the rice into the jar first, it will prevent all of the walnuts from having enough room to fit. However, if you put all of your walnuts into the jar first, and then begin to sprinkle in the rice, you will see the rice fits nicely around the crevices of the walnuts. In accomplishing the task in this fashion, you will indeed be able to get all of the original contents back into the jar. In fact – the ONLY WAY to get everything back into that jar is to insert the contents in the proper order. **If it is done in proper order… it will all fit properly.**

This is a great analogy for prioritizing the activities of your business. If you execute the most urgent and important activities first (dollar producing activities), you will have plenty of time to accomplish the less urgent and less important tasks, afterward. You will also feel a sense of accomplishment, and have closure to your day. **How**

different would your business look if you could execute your dollar producing activities first, every day, and have clarity of priorities for executing the less urgent tasks later?

In this section, you will identify what your walnuts (key activities) are. I will provide you with the tools needed to help you stay on track to accomplish the execution of those key activities. Then, as you execute those key activities every day and every week, you can begin to sprinkle in those ancillary tasks (your rice). By the end of the day, the week, or the month, you will find that the promise – "you can get everything done that NEEDS to get done" will be the truth, not a pipe dream.

How the CORE Weekly Action Plan Works

The key word for this tool is "static." The CORE Weekly Action Plan is a STATIC list of things that you have identified as important tasks and activities you would like to do consistently every day and every week to move your business forward. (It is a STATIC list of your "walnuts.")

This form is NOT a daily task list. Instead, this is **a list of key activities that rarely change**. You will keep this form visible in your immediate workspace. You will reference it throughout the day and week to remind you of what your key priorities are. This very simple but powerful tool will help you stay on course to the attainment of your goals. In fact, **The CORE Weekly Action Plan is one of the single most powerful elements of your system.**

How do I know that? My experience with top producers is that almost all of them have an organized way to maximize their use of time. It is a common attribute for most of them. They know what they must accomplish each day, week and month, **and they have a system to get it done**. On the other hand, less experienced or less productive sales professionals tend to have an undisciplined, haphazard approach to organization. *Their income reflects their level of discipline.* The results of our survey supported our day-to-day observations:

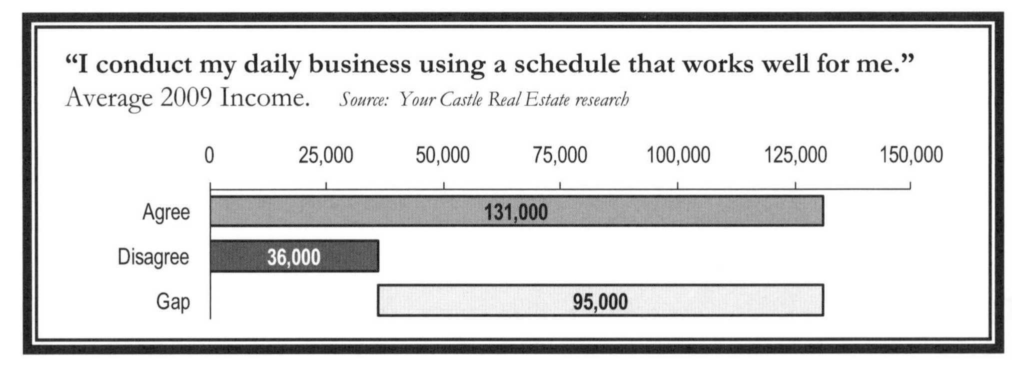

How can you bring this degree of clarity to YOUR business?

Think it through… for YOU

To start establishing your *personalized* CORE Weekly Action Plan, you will want to brainstorm the key activities that move your business forward. Here are a few ideas to get you started:

Daily	Weekly	Monthly
Handle urgent email Return urgent phone calls Follow up with prospects Schedule Appointments Social Media	Execute Marketing Campaigns Complete a specific number of appointments	Plan marketing campaigns Database Management Quantitative Measurements of Results

Now, take a few moments to begin to fill in the form below with some of your key STATIC activities.

Daily	Weekly	Monthly

Another CORE Key – Your Standards of Professional Excellence

Another important component to your CORE Weekly Action Plan is establishing three to five standards of Professional Excellence. These standards should reflect social graces, professional courtesies and habitual ways of working that you want to demonstrate on a daily basis. Here are a few examples:

- "I return all of my incoming calls the same business day."
- "I respond to any important emails I receive before 5 pm, even if it is simply to let them know when I will get back to them."
- "I follow up with each lead I receive within 24 hours.

To identify your standards of excellence, ask yourself:

- "What is important to me when I am on the receiving end of service?"
- "What kind of attention and service level do I expect or most appreciate?"
- "What attitude or service attribute do I find most desirable in my service providers that I would like to adopt as my own?"

Take a few moments and write some ideas down:

1. ____

2. ____

3. ____

4. ____

5. ____

The CORE Weekly Action Plan

I have developed this tool so you have one place to record all of this information as a STATIC document you can quickly reference every day.

- Some people put this form on a bulletin board to use as a visual reference only
- Others put this form into their Operations Manual (one of the tools shared in Chapter 7, Piles to Files). They use the check boxes provided to mark off their daily and weekly accomplishments.
- Others create a large poster out of this form, laminate it and hang it on their office wall. By laminating it, they can use the check boxes to mark off the items they are accomplishing daily and weekly with a wet-erase pen.
- Others have a digital version of this form or an electronic way to track and execute all of these items.

The bottom line: this form is designed to be a "week at a glance" reference sheet, and however you elect to use this concept is up to you. The CORE Weekly Action Plan can be downloaded from my website: www.EfficiencyByDesignOnline.com.

Below is the complete form as I have designed it. Take a moment to renew this document and absorb this concept. I will be walking you through the individual sections one element at a time.

MY CORE ACTION PLAN

CENTER ON RESULTS EVERY DAY

MY STANDARDS OF PROFESSIONAL EXCELLENCE

1. ______________________________
2. ______________________________
3. ______________________________
4. ______________________________
5. ______________________________

DAILY DISCIPLINES	WEEKLY DISCIPLINES
Focus on SETTING UP YOUR DAY **Time Block: Daily Prep** ☐☐☐☐☐ A Priority Emails ☐☐☐☐☐ A Priority Phone Calls ☐☐☐☐☐ Daily EMarketing Responsibilities ☐☐☐☐☐ Check "A" Folders – Email /Digital & Paper ☐☐☐☐☐ ______________ ☐☐☐☐☐ ______________	**WEEKLY SALES & VISABILITY FOCUS:** **"How am I ACTIVELY meeting new people this week?"** Consider community involvement, socializing, service & volunteer work, hobbies and interests, political. ☐ ______________ ☐ ______________
Focus on NEW BUSINESS: **Time Block: Happy Hour** ☐☐☐☐☐ Reference my HOT SHEET & Other lead sources. (See below) ☐☐☐☐☐ Make ____phone calls daily & update database with my actions and conversations ✓✓✓✓✓✓✓ Scheduled appointments for this week **My Lead Sources**: Just Met, Referred, A Prospects, Referrals , ______________	**WEEKLY MARKETING FOCUS:** **" How am I PASSIVELY staying connected this week?"** ☐ ______________ ☐ ______________ ☐ ______________ ☐ Update Social Media Sites ☐ Update Website & Blog
Focus on CURRENT BUSINESS/OPEN FILES **Time Block: Current Transactions** ☐☐☐☐☐ - Reference The Parking Lot* ☐☐☐☐☐ Proactively contact my current clients ☐☐☐☐☐ Proactively connect with the service providers on my open files. ☐☐☐☐☐ ______________ ☐☐☐☐☐ ______________	**PROJECTS & PLANNING** **"What projects am I working on this week to position myself more effectively?"** (Consider marketing campaigns, presentation improvements, strategic planning, etc.) ☐ ______________ **"Things I need to do to plan and prepare for next week:"** ☐ Print Daily Pages for next week. ☐ Plan for next week. ☐ Database Maintenance- Qualify & Categorize ☐ Determine who I will call next week ☐ Update my HOT SHEET* for next week.
STOP THE MOMENTUM. "Wrap it up…." **Time Block: Completions & Deliverables** ☐☐☐☐☐ Follow up from today's appointments ☐☐☐☐☐ Update database with new contacts ☐☐☐☐☐ Respond to "B-Email" ☐☐☐☐☐ Plan for tomorrow ☐☐☐☐☐ ______________ Daily Recap: ☐☐☐☐☐ How many connections today? ☐☐☐☐☐ On a scale of 1-10, how would I rate myself today?	**WEEKLY RECAP:** ________ Prospecting Appointments ________ New Presentations ________ Past Client Connections ________ Closed Business ________ Accountability call or meeting

- * You will read more about these items shortly.

- **MY CORE ACTION PLAN**
- CENTER ON RESULTS EVERY DAY

Let's discuss the overall layout of the CORE Weekly Action Plan.

The very top of this form lists your Standards of Professional Excellence	
The Left Side Represents **Daily CORE Activities** (Daily Disciplines)	The Right Side Represents **Weekly CORE Activities** (Weekly Disciplines)
Focus on SETTING UP YOUR DAY **Time Block: Daily Prep** This section lists your Daily Prep activities, which you completed in **the first 30-minute time block** of your day.	**WEEKLY SALES & VISABILITY FOCUS:** **"How am I ACTIVELY meeting new people this week?"** This section gives you the space to jot down what you plan to do this week to create visibility for yourself and actively meet new people.
Focus on NEW BUSINESS: **Time Block: Happy Hour** This section helps you to focus on your coveted "Happy Hour." Happy Hour is **one allotted hour of PHONE WORK ONLY**. It is about making calls to set appointments, including follow-up with active prospects. (We explore this in more detail in Chapter 10, "Mastering the Art of Follow-Up.")	**WEEKLY MARKETING FOCUS:** **" How am I PASSIVELY staying connected this week?"** This section gives you the space to write down what you will do to passively connect this week with the people in your network. Quick, passive connections are executed during the Daily Prep time block. More time intensive passive connections should be executed during Projects and Planning time.
Focus on CURRENT BUSINESS/OPEN FILES **Time Block: Current Transactions** The section helps you stay aware of "Current Transactions." It includes a list of activities to help you stay on top of your current business and make sure your deals are on track to close. For the traditional sales professionals who has staff handling production, I recommend **an hour or less be given to this activity** daily. Sales professionals who are also responsible for production will need to make more time for this segment, but should never sacrifice their "Happy Hour."	**PROJECTS & PLANNING** This section offers a quick way to identify projects you want to accomplish this week. It also gives you a checklist of activities to complete to prepare you for the following week so you can hit the ground running. Projects are executed during Projects and Planning time.
STOP THE MOMENTUM. "Wrap it up…." **Time Block: Completions & Deliverables** This section reminds to you "stop working and start wrapping up." The checklist reflects what you need to finish to feel complete for the day. There are also a few questions you can answer to evaluate your day. **I suggest slotting about 1-2 hours at the end of your day for Completions and Deliverables.**	**WEEKLY RECAP:** This section allows you to take a moment to recap the current week's results. Tracking your business results is an important part of staying CORE. This can be executed during Completions and Deliverables, or Projects and Planning.

Make the CORE Weekly Action Plan your **KEY PRODUCTIVITY TOOL.**

Once you download this form, make any changes you need to in order to establish this as **your key productivity tool**. To gain further clarity as to the use of this form, let's look at each of the sections in a little more detail:

Focus on SETTING UP YOUR DAY
Time Block: Daily Prep

☐☐☐☐☐☐ A Priority Email s
☐☐☐☐☐☐ A Priority Phone Calls
☐☐☐☐☐☐ Daily EMarketing Responsibilities
☐☐☐☐☐☐ Check "A" Folders – Email /Digital & Paper
☐☐☐☐☐☐ ____________________
☐☐☐☐☐☐ ____________________

Daily Prep

While you may get over a hundred emails a day, only a few will be "A" Priority. This tracking box reminds you to address only those "A" Priority emails at the beginning of your day that arrived during the evening. You accomplish this during your Daily Prep Time to which you are only allotting about 30 minutes. Handle "A" priority phone calls the same way. Of course, calls and emails will continue to pour in throughout the day. Respond only to those that are "A" Priority. Respond to "B" priority calls and emails to at the end of your day during your Completions and Deliverables time.

WEEKLY SALES & VISABILITY FOCUS:
"How am I ACTIVELY meeting new people?"

Consider community involvement, socializing, service & volunteer work, hobbies and interests, political.

☐ ____________________
☐ ____________________

Weekly Sales & Visibility Focus

This tracking box reflects what activities you are engaged in this week to meet new prospects. Using the example, let's say you want to make $100,000 per year and need 125 great relationships to generate that income (see next section: Happy Hour). If you only have 40 strong client or referral relationships, one of your main tasks should be to increase the size of your network. If you are still in the early stages of your career, where you are "building a book of business", you will want to think about networking opportunities here. Perhaps you can make a commitment to attend at least one networking event each week.

Happy Hour

Many-a-sales-trainer has a different name for this important time of your day. You may have heard it referred to as Hour of Power or The Power Hour. The bottom line is that it is coveted time for you **to schedule appointments for this week and next week**. It is about phone work, ONLY.

Focus on NEW BUSINESS:
Time Block: Happy Hour

☐☐☐☐☐ Reference my HOT SHEET & Other lead sources. (See below)
☐☐☐☐☐ Make ____phone calls daily & update database with my actions and conversations

✓✓✓✓✓✓✓ Scheduled appointments for this week
My Lead Sources: Just Met, Referred, A Prospects, Referrals ,
____

It is a good idea to know how many people you need to have in your network to make the amount of money you want to make on an annual basis. For example, a Realtor can use the general rule of thumb that they will make $800 - $1000 per person per year with whom they have a good relationship. That means if they want to make $100,000, they will need 100-125 contacts. If you need to talk to each person six times a year, that's 750 calls over a year. If you work five days a week, fifty weeks a year, that's 250 work days. You need to make three (750 calls divided by 250 work days) client relationship calls per day.

Your network and industry will have different requirements, so think this one through. Then determine a target number of calls you need to make per day, and the number of appointments you need to set weekly to accomplish your goals.

Use the small boxes on this form to check off the days that you engage in Happy Hour. Use the checkmarks to remind you how many appointments you need to set for the week and then circle the checkmarks as you set them. If you are making calls on Monday to set appointments for this week and next week, your goal is to have all of these check marks circled before Tuesday even arrives. You can add more check marks to this form, or any other information you deem important to remember during your Happy Hour. I have also included a list of lead sources to remind you where you can find the contacts needed to accomplish the number of calls you will be making to get to your goal.

Weekly Marketing Focus

In the Chapter 10, "Mastering the Art of Follow-Up," I talk about using passive marketing campaigns to stay in touch with interested prospects who are just not ready to buy today. You need to stay in touch with them to keep your sales pipeline full. Use this box to plan and track the activities related to your passive marketing.

> **WEEKLY MARKETING FOCUS:**
> **" How am I PASSIVELY staying connected?"**
>
> ☐ ______________________
>
> ☐ ______________________
>
> ☐ ______________________
>
> ☐ Update Social Media Sites
> ☐ Update Website & Blog

One of the authors sends out a weekly e-newsletter and a monthly paper newsletter. The weekly communication highlights upcoming training events and workshops. The monthly newsletter talks about market trends and industry developments. Some of this content also ends up in their blog and, in short a "teaser" form, and some social media sites. (After you complete Chapter 10, you will have a number of ideas for your passive marketing.)

Current Business/Open Files

Some sales professionals stay involved with their deals to some degree until they are officially closed. This section of the form reminds you to take a moment and look into how things are progressing. It suggests you proactively communicate with any service providers also involved in this transaction. The more proactive you are in making calls on current transactions, the fewer incoming calls you will receive... and the more efficient your day will be.

> **Focus on CURRENT BUSINESS/OPEN FILES**
> **Time Block: Current Transactions**
>
> ☐☐☐☐☐ Proactively contact my current clients
>
> ☐☐☐☐☐ Proactively connect with the service providers on my open files.
>
> ☐☐☐☐☐ ______________________
>
> ☐☐☐☐☐ ______________________

Projects and Planning

What projects will you be working on this week to get them prepare them for implementation into your business? Add them to your tracking box.

The bottom suggests the activities you might complete near the end of the week to prepare for a fast start the following Monday morning. Add anything here that helps you stay organized in this way.

> **PROJECTS & PLANNING**
> **"What projects am I working on to position myself more effectively?** (Consider marketing campaigns, presentation improvements, strategic planning, etc.)
> ☐ ______________________
>
> **"Things I need to do to plan and prepare for next week:"**
> ☐ Print Daily Pages for next week.
> ☐ Plan for next week.
> ☐ Database Maintenance- Qualify & Categorize
> ☐ Determine who I will call next week
> ☐ Update my HOT SHEET.

Stop the Momentum. "Wrap it Up..."

The ending of your workday is just as critical as the beginning of it. There are certain things you want to do at the end of every day that will allow you to feel a degree of completion (or accomplishment!) before heading for home. The last few hours of the day are the time to execute those actions.

- Have you promised your prospects and clients any deliverables or follow up on the discussion to advance the relationship to the next level? Handle that during this time slot.
- Have you made new connections today and need to add their contact information and conversation notes to your database and passive marketing campaigns? This is the time to do it.

You scheduled some follow-up appointments today. Get them into your calendar. Plan for tomorrow. Respond to any "B" priority calls and emails that were not high on your list to respond to over the course of the day.

STOP THE MOMENTUM. "Wrap it up…."
Time Block: Completions & Deliverables

☐☐☐☐☐ Follow up from today's appointments
☐☐☐☐☐ Update database with new contacts
☐☐☐☐☐ Respond to "B-Email"
☐☐☐☐☐ Plan for tomorrow
☐☐☐☐☐ ______________________________

Daily Recap:
☐☐☐☐☐ How many connections today?
☐☐☐☐☐ On a scale of 1-10, how would I rate myself today?

Take it from someone who knows. Your completions and deliverables hour is **essential for a well-functioning sales business**. These items will keep you up at night if you do not tend to them during this slotted time. Lost opportunities occur because sales professionals do not slow down long enough to take the time to follow up and handle these items at the end of their day. If you are like me, you may actually need incentive to "stop working". When I am running one hundred miles an hour and find myself missing my Completions and Deliverables time, I will occasionally end my day around 3 and head for my home office to wrap things up. I have control over my environment there and can get a huge amount of work done in a very short period. Execute these deliverables in an environment that allows for unplugging and relaxation while wrapping things up. You are in sales, so take advantage of the control you have regarding when and where you handle things! Your pocket book will thank you.

A HUGE note of caution: In case you need additional incentive to make sure your completions and deliverables time occurs, consider this: If you do not execute these wrap up items in the evening, you will be forced to execute them in the morning. More than likely, your morning time is your most dollar productive time to call and set appointments, or meet with prospects and clients. That means, if you are executing these deliverables in the morning, you are destroying your most important dollar productive hours with non-dollar productive activities. Think about how much that can negatively affect your business. Get your completions and deliverables done in the evening. Do not procrastinate.

A recap of how well you feel you worked today is included in this section of the CORE Weekly Action Plan. You can jot down your "score" in the small boxes. This helps you see any patterns that may be occurring. More than likely, the days you made the most new connections will probably be the days you feel you worked at "level 10". This scoring system helps you see how energizing it really is to meet new people, work efficiently, and live your plan.

WEEKLY RECAP:

________ Prospecting Appointments
________ New Presentations
________ Past Client Connections
________ Closed Business

________ Accountability call or meeting

<u>**Weekly Disciplines – Weekly Recap**</u>

One of the authors wraps up the week by summarizing their successes. It is also helpful to compare some of the key metrics (such as the number of completed appointments) to the target in the overall business plan.

Consider which items would be helpful in measuring in your business and add them to this tracking box..

B: The Parking Lot

We are what we repeatedly do. Excellence, therefore, is not an act, but a habit.
Aristotle

The Parking Lot tool allows you to jot down good ideas that come to mind, and save them in a safe place until you can further process them. Write all of your ideas in one place instead of on post-it notes and note pads in many different places. This reduces the risk of losing ideas. You do not have to prioritize the items in your Parking Lot. You can pull ideas from The Parking Lot into your daily process and ninety day action plan as your day-to-day schedule permits.

Sales professionals frequently have a notebook they carry around with them to jot down conversation notes or ideas as they arise. Other sales professionals may use a white board. We absolutely need our Parking Lot, and most of us already have one. Unfortunately, many of us have more than one, and that is where we run into problems. For example, we may have a journal, but end up acquiring scratch paper, loose paper lists, sticky notes, note cards, or in extreme cases napkins, coasters, or the back of our own business cards. In the case of The Parking Lot, "more" is not the merrier… it is an organizational nightmare.

> *"I try to leave specific blocks of time alone so they can work as slush zones. If something interesting does pop up, it does not throw me off track."*
>
> Quote from survey

Another challenge: important ideas we write down tend to get lost very easily within the pages of our Parking Lot. Many people do not allocate time at the end of the day to reference their notes and set up follow-up activities. We are frequently running to our next appointment and failing to provide deliverables to our clients. The failure point of The Parking Lot: not referencing or transferring the information (or task) to a more structured tool that will ensure our follow-up. Then we lose the momentum of the relationships we have worked so hard to establish.

Using Your Parking Lot

The key to efficiency is **moving** the information from The Parking Lot into our other tools – such as our calendars, task lists, databases, project folders, or business plans. As you begin to move information from your Parking Lots into these tools, remove the item from the Parking Lot by either throwing away the note, or crossing a line through the item. Part of your static to-do list each day should include a few minutes for you to perform this activity, best executed during your completions and deliverables time, or in some cases, project time.

Multiple Parking Lots

If your Parking Lot is unmanageable, or if you have multiple parking lots, I have created two tools that will assist you in organizing your thoughts and your tasks. If you condense everything into one place, you can more easily comprehend *all* of your ideas and begin to prioritize them into manageable, executable tasks.

The tools are:

- The Condenser
- The Portable Project Board

Process to handle multiple Parking Lots

1. Visit www.EfficiencyByDesignOnline.com.
2. Download The Condenser and The Portable Project Board.
3. Gather all of your floating sticky notes and put them into a pile.
4. Gather all of your multiple tasks lists and put them into a pile
5. Organize your notes and task lists into The Condenser.
6. Sort tasks into three columns: tomorrow, this week and this month.

Condense Your Tasks Lists & Sticky Notes

Tomorrow	This Week	This Month

Place anything else that you plan to accomplish beyond the current month onto the "The Portable Project Board".

The Portable Project Board
Use this form to capture project ideas or "C Priority" Tasks you do not want to lose.

Project Ideas	"C Priority" Tasks

Refer back to the "Condenser."Identify when you must complete urgent tasks: tomorrow, this week or this month. Jot those items down on your Daily Planning Pages (see Tool "C" in this chapter).

As you adopt your new system, it will become a habit for you to move Parking Lot notes to your calendars, task lists, databases, project folders, etc. You may find you use the Portable Project board consistently, and are able to avoid multiple lists or sticky notes piling up. However, when you feel you are getting out of control with tasks lists, sticky notes or Parking Lot ideas, return to this process. You will enjoy the feeling of control you get from prioritizing all of your floating ideas!

C: The Daily Planning Pages

Discipline is the bridge between goals and accomplishment.
Jim Rohn

Your CORE Weekly Action Plan (tool "A" in this chapter) is *static*, whereas your daily Planning Pages are flowing and *dynamic*. These pages are your "Task List" the list of the things you need to accomplish *today and this week*. You should prioritize this list in the order of *importance of execution*. The key word in this tool is DYNAMIC. All of us have experienced establishing a list of daily priorities, only to find ourselves thrown off track when a crisis occurs (either real, or perceived to be a crisis by an important client). It is perfectly acceptable to give yourself permission to switch gears, but only if the demand is a legitimately urgent one. The Daily Planning Pages will help you to switch gears consciously.

> *"Prioritize tasks by A, B, C lists. Knowing what is most important or needs immediate attention will help me not to be caught up in the less important tasks."*
>
> Quote from survey

How to Plan

I suggest taking time at the end of your day to plan for the next day. If you do this, your chances of hitting the ground running are substantially higher…as are your chances of sleeping at night. Personally, I print out seven daily planning pages at one time and keep them in my Operations Manual (See Chapter 7, Piles to Files). Once you have identified what tasks are urgent that **must be accomplished** tomorrow and the remaining days of this week, you will want to jot those down on your Daily Planning Pages.

Most efficiency experts agree that selecting more than five "A Priority" tasks is efficiency suicide. I agree. If it appears you have more than five, it is essential that you choose five that you MUST complete today "or else" … and work diligently to accomplish them as quickly and efficiently as possible.

Remember that the items you want to list on your Daily Planning Pages are tasks not already included in your static CORE Weekly Action Plan. You do not need to jot down CORE actions on your Daily Planning Pages. You already have those items on your radar.

I have designed some daily planning pages that fit perfectly with the Efficiency by Design Time Mastery system we outlined in Chapter 6. Below is a screen shot of the daily forms that are available for your use, downloadable from my website. Directions on how to use this are included on the form. This tool reflects your time mastery method from Chapter 6.

The Daily Planning Pages

Time Block:

PREP Daily Prep
TRAN Current Transaction
COMP Completions & Deliverables
$ $ $ Appointments/Presentations
CALL Hour of Power
EVE Work to accomplish after 5pm
PRO Projects & Planning
PSNL Personal Task

Priority:

A **ABSOLUTELY must be done today**
B **Do BEFORE week end**
C **COULD be done before month end**

Action:

✓ **Completed**
X **Eliminated**
→ **Forwarded**
***** **Delegated/Pending**
MT **Moved to Master Tasks**

1. Jot down your task. 2. Prioritize as A, B or C 3. Indicate the associated time block. 4. TAKE ACTION!

ABC	BLOCK	✓	Task:

D: The Appointment Calendar

> *If you are going to achieve excellence in big things, you develop the habit in little matters. Excellence is not an exception; it is a prevailing attitude.*
> Colin Powell

I have purposefully not established an appointment calendaring system, because this is such a personal subject. Some of us prefer paper, some electronic. Some prefer to view our appointments by day, others by week or month. Some like large calendars, some like smaller ones. Many sales professionals use software specifically geared toward this end. The main thing is to have a system… and use it.

All of the authors use Outlook. Many of our clients do, too. For clients without a system, I recommend they utilize this universally accepted calendar and contact management system. It is especially powerful if you have a Blackberry and you can synchronize Outlook to your device.

The functionality of your appointment calendar is to help you reference your availability for meetings. It also needs to help you protect your personal time, prospecting time, and project time. In order for your calendar to be an effective tool in your business that works for you, you will want to make sure it reflects two specific things:

(1) Your SCHEDULED daily, weekly, monthly meetings and appointments

(2) Your PRE-DETERMINED time blocked commitments, such as daily prep, Happy Hour, Completions and Deliverables.

Electronic Calendars

I have included below a screen shot of my own Outlook Calendar to show you how I visually create a time blocking system that allows me to pre-block reoccurring appointments I set for "my business" and record new appointments I set with others. It is VERY freeing to be able to pre-fill my calendar with reoccurrence options with the time blocks I have already predetermined as the best way for me to spend my time. Of course, because I am in sales, I also want to give myself permission to make conscious decisions and make changes as necessary. Having it all down here in black and white – or color as is the case with my specific system - is incredibly helpful.

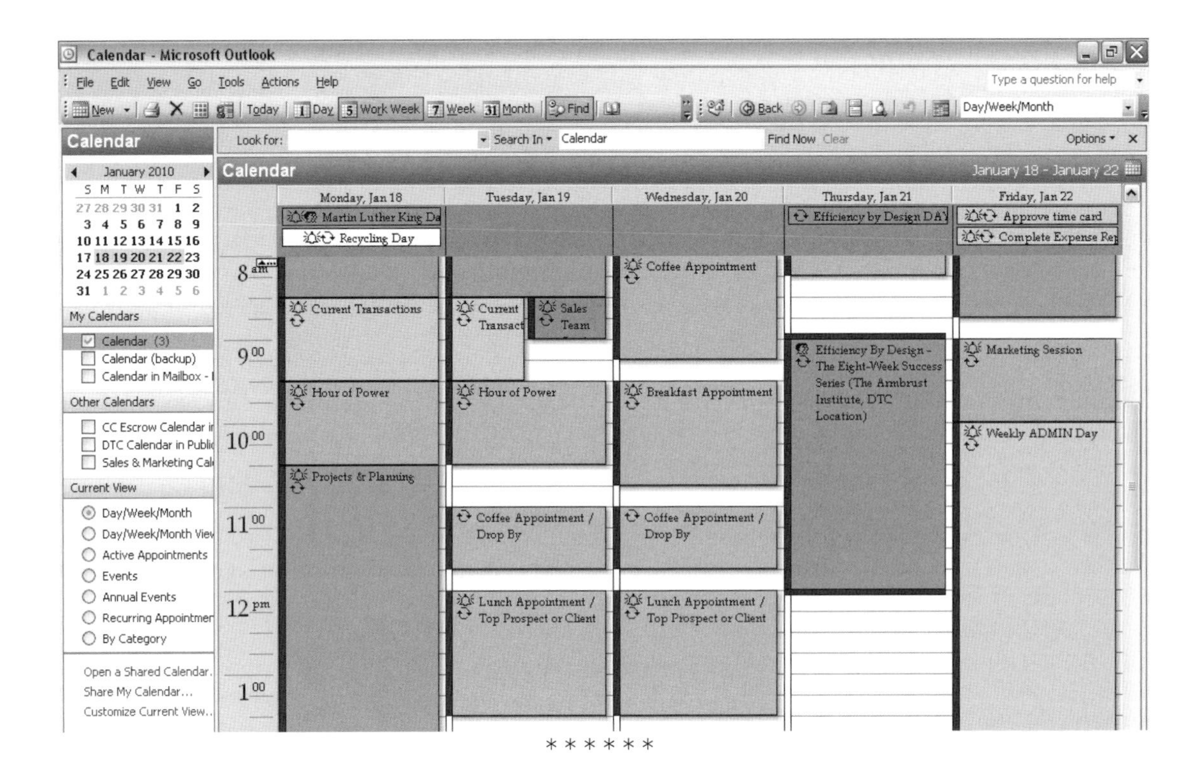

* * * * * *

Implementation

Wasn't that interesting to read? We need to move you from having been interested to taking action. Make the commitment to improve your business.

My Commitment to My Business

- I will TAKE ACTION to make a difference in my business, TODAY!
- I stay CORE (Centered on Results Every Day).
- I EXECUTE what I am learning. I am not a perpetual student.

My greatest "AHA!" moments from this chapter were:

____

____

____

My 24 hour Commitment is (what idea related to this chapter can I implement in 24 hours):

____

____

____

My Seven Day Commitment is:

____

____

____

My new standard of professional excellence or habitual way of working is:

____

____

____

* * * * * *

What does success look like?
It's important to note that if you are doing **the majority** of the things suggested in this chapter **the majority** of the time, THAT IS SUCCESS. It's not possible to do all things, all of the time. But if you can honestly look at yourself and say that you are doing what you need to be doing about 51% of the time, that is success.

What is in the next chapter?
Do you feel like you have a handle on Daily Disciplines? The next secret of highly efficient sales professionals is revealed in Chapter 9, "Falling in Love with Your Database." Recall that CORE stands for "Center on Results Every Day." In Chapter 9 you will learn:

A. Why even bother with a database?
B. Why should I fall in love with my database?
C. Categorizing versus qualifying leads
D. How do I manage all of the business cards?
E. Implementation

I would recommend investing some time in this chapter if you scored a B or below on your assessment in Database Management.

9. Falling in Love with Your Database

"As with any relationship… you get out of it what you put into it."

Three things that never come back: the spent arrow; the spoken word; the lost opportunity.
William Paige

This quote was very significant for this chapter. For many sales professionals, the database is a basket filled with lost opportunities. This chapter outlines ways to capture and follow up with each new business opportunity that crosses your path. Following the steps in the chapter will increase your sales effectiveness in your business and make your database a powerful tool.

How Does "Falling in Love with Your Database" Fit Into the System?

There are four Cornerstones of success. You do not necessarily need to master each of them to move on to the more advanced concepts. However, before moving on, you should be able to answer at least "neutral" instead of "disagree" on most of the Cornerstone questions on the survey in the beginning of the book.

This chapter will help you understand:

A. Why even bother with a database?
B. Why should I "fall in love" with my database?
C. Categorizing versus qualifying leads
D. "How do I manage all of these business cards?"
E. Implementation

When you finish "Database Skills," you will progress to "Mastering the Art of Follow-Up," which builds on your skills.

Why Even Bother with a Database?

My experience with top producers is that almost all of them have a methodical way of tracking and qualifying their past clients and their current prospects. It is a common attribute for most of them. Less productive sales professionals tend to use their database in a limited fashion – a glorified

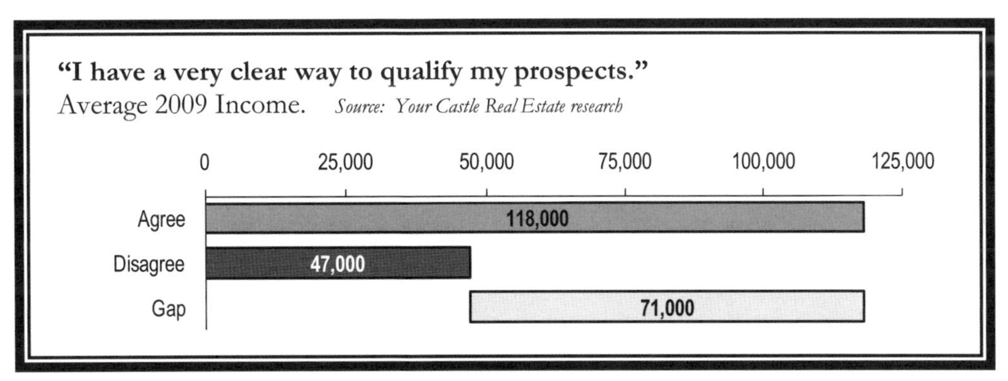

rolodex. Income clearly reflects commitment. Our survey supported our day-to-day observations on the importance of a well-maintained database:

The sales professionals who strongly agreed they have a clear way of qualifying prospects made more than twice as much as those who disagreed with the statement.

In another survey question, we asked about the challenges sales professionals face with their prospecting activities and their database.. Following are a few other responses that we received:

- "I have too many old leads. I send market updates to them all but I have over 11,000 in my database." (Income over $100K)
- "It is a constant challenge sorting and qualifying my database." (Income over $100K)
- "Keeping it [my database] up to date and communicating on a regular basis." (Income over $100K)

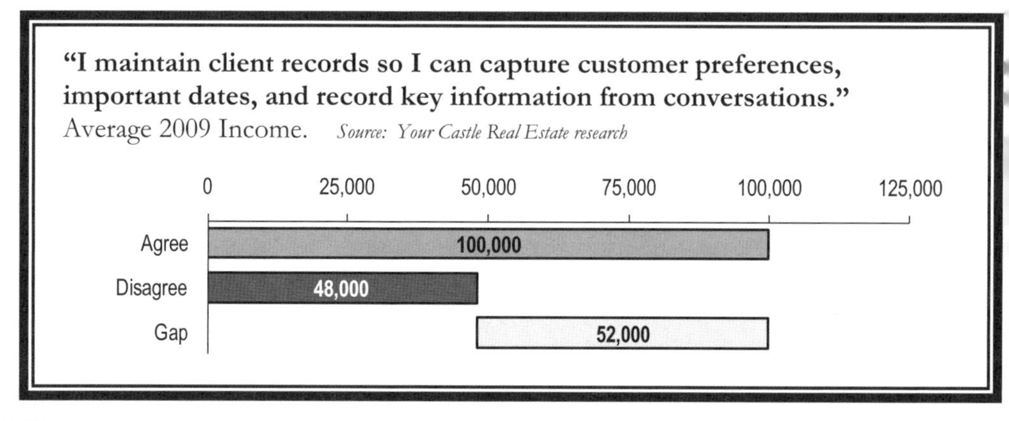

Have you experienced similar challenges and frustrations? If so, this chapter will have many ideas to help you. We asked one other question on the survey that relates to your use of a database:

Here are some of the comments received for the question, "What challenges do you face with client records?"

- "I need better technology and skills... I just lack the tools, and cannot afford more up to date stuff."
- "I have a hard time reviewing it [my database] on a regular basis."

Here are some of the comments we received for the question, "What is working well for you with client records?"

- "My database is categorized so I can sort as needed." (Income over $100K)
- "My online database keeps me very organized. I have an A, B and C [priority] system for classifying leads."
- "I enter as much info as I can into my Blackberry that is then synced with Outlook and I can fill in the missing bits of info later."
- "I use Outlook categories to help me send the right information to the right people."

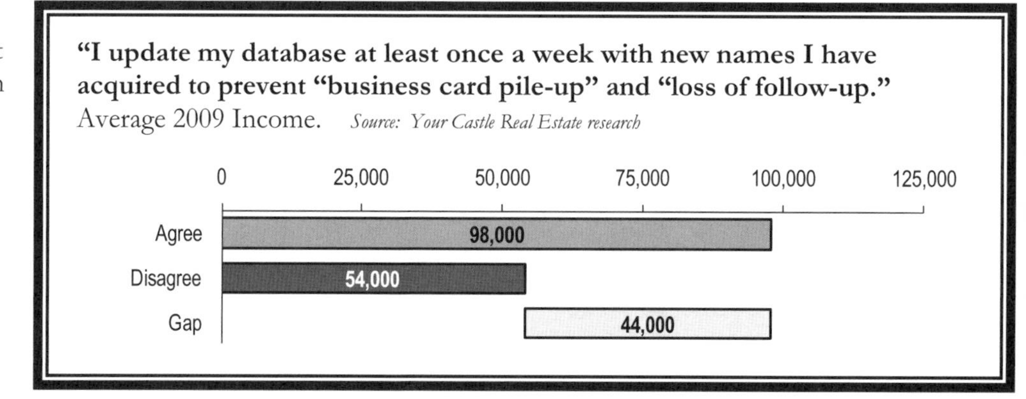

Finally, we asked, "What challenges do you face with keeping your database current?"

- "Getting the information entered quickly after each contact while the information is still fresh."
- "Time to stay on top of it [entered new leads into the database] without pile-up."

We also asked, "What is working well for you?" One sample response:

- "Only enter real leads into it [the database] and do not worry about the rest." (Income over $100K)

> *"I periodically run through the entire database and look at names to see if there is someone I should contact, or may want to increase in priority, or delete. When you only have one letter (of the last name) to do for the day, it makes it manageable as opposed to being overwhelmed with your whole database. I have 2,000 names, so I cannot run through that many at a time."*
>
> Quote from survey; income over $100K)

Regardless of your industry, you will make more money with a well-organized database. Perhaps as importantly, you will be in control of your business. If you are a business owner, you will be on your way to creating a business you can sell when you retire… versus having to work until you collapse.

Why Should I Fall in Love with My Database?

Just in case you need further evidence as to how important your database REALLY is for your business, let's examine a few of the roles that your database plays in establishing your sales success. When used correctly, your database will:

- Be an effective tool to help you communicate efficiently with your network.
- Keep you connected with your past clients to cultivate referral business.
- Help you identify where your next deal is coming from.

Getting Acquainted with Your Database

Following is an insightful exercise that allows you to see the real value of your database. List three adjectives or short phrases that describe the current condition of your database:

1. ______________________________

2. ______________________________

3. ______________________________

Now, list three adjectives or short phrases that describe the condition of your sales business:

1. ______________________________

2. ______________________________

3. ______________________________

What are your observations from this exercise?

____

____

____

For most sales professionals, there is a mirror effect between these two lists. Frequently, the condition of their database reflects perfectly the condition of their business. Do you see yourself in this scenario? Can you see how important it is to accurately create, update and maintain your database records? There is a close relationship between the quality of database and your earnings. When teaching classes about building a better database, I often I ask my students to complete this sentence:

"My database WANTS to _______________.

I enjoy having them "fill in the blank," and they have come up with some very clever and sincere responses. Some samples: My database wants to…

- Make me wealthy
- Pick up where my child support payment has left off
- Keep me out of debt
- Have a faster computer and a better house to live in
- Get some exercise! I haven't used it for years!
- Keep me organized and more efficient.
- Love me
- Get some attention.
- Be a database, not a rolodex!

So, knowing all of the fabulous things your database wants to do for you, what have you just discovered about *your* database?

You **must** establish a loving and connected relationship with your database! Always remember… as with any relationship, you get out of it what you put into it!

"I thought you'd be interested to know that I am SERIOUSLY dating my database tonight. My husband is gone and we are having some ALONE time! We are even going to call Microsoft Outlook Support!

Just thought I would let you know you have me inspired! "

A salesperson that participated in the pilot efficiency classes

Cultivating a Monogamous, Long-Term Relationship with Your Database:

Research what software choices are available out there for you. There are so many systems from which to choose. Some are more attractive than others. Some are dysfunctional, some are hard to understand and work with, some are too expensive or high maintenance and not worth the trouble. (Interesting parallels, yes?)

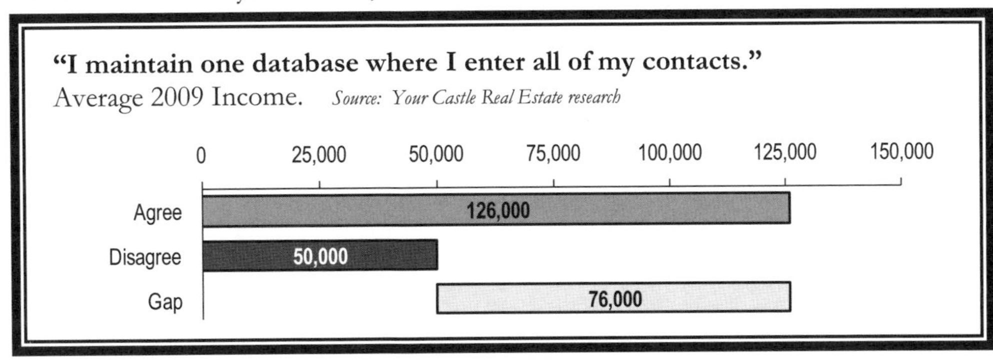

Does the monogamy pay off? It certainly did for the sales people in our survey.

The Exclusive Phase

You have seen what is out there, so now it is time to get exclusive. Select ONE database with which you will establish a long-term, monogamous relationship. Once you have selected "the one," you have to give it everything you've got! Condense every other address book, email address lists, Excel spreadsheet, all of your cell phone numbers… everything into this tool.

What if you are like the sales person that wrote this comment on the survey?

> "*[My challenge is] Keeping it [my database] up to date and communicating on a regular basis.*"
> (Income over $100K)

Consider hiring someone to help you set up your database and do the initial data loading. Once it is set up, if you spend a few minutes on it each day (or at least weekly), keeping it up to date should not take that much time or effort.

Staying Monogamous

Do not be tempted to stray! There are so many other dazzling databases out there that can catch your eye and tempt you. However, each time you change your database, you have to deal with all of the quirks and questions the new one brings. Honor your time and money investment and stick with only one database. You made a commitment. Make it work.

There are also services that will trick you into thinking they should be your database. However, you must remember that those services are just that: services! A service will to help you with marketing. Your database will tell you where your next deal is coming from. A service is not a customer relationship management software – it is just a service to help you reach out and market to your sphere.

> What is a marketing service vs. what is your database?
>
> *Here is how you can tell the difference. Something you can upload an excel spreadsheet into and email blast out of, or will use your excel to send postcards or newsletters out on your behalf is only a service.*

Do not fall into the trap of updating these "services" first and then neglecting to enter those names into your database. Make your database "your everything." Make your database "the mother ship," and export information *from* your database into those other services as needed.

Allow for a Mutually Beneficial Relationship
This is, hands-down, the easiest relationship you will ever have. Your database does not need flowers or candy or a night out with the boys. It just wants NAMES and NEW CONNECTIONS! Your database is very sad when you are sitting at your computer working away and it sees the stacks of business cards wrapped in a rubber band sitting next to the monitor (You know the stack I am talking about). Your database wants to help you with communication, follow up and follow through. How can it help you if you do not first provide it with the information it needs?

Deepen Your Communication
It is BEST if your database can synchronize with your phone so you have a constant thread of communication wherever you go. Some of you will have a deeper level of communication than others with your database. If your cell phone does not synchronize with your database, you can still have a nice relationship with it. However, you will find the deepest relationship will come when there is a deeper connection through a syncing function.

Categorizing versus Qualifying Leads

In my system, a "category" tells you HOW you met someone or WHAT their hobbies and interests are. Chapter 11 will share more about the importance of answering the question of "WHAT." A "qualification" tells you WHEN you anticipate they will convert from a prospect to a client. One critical error many sales people make – regardless of industry – is adding names to their databases, categorizing them, and then *not continuing with the qualification process*! You MUST QUALIFY each person as to WHEN you anticipate they will convert from prospect to client. If all you do is categorize your database, it cannot help you generate new business or identify where your next deal is coming from.

Does it matter financially? Here is what the survey found:

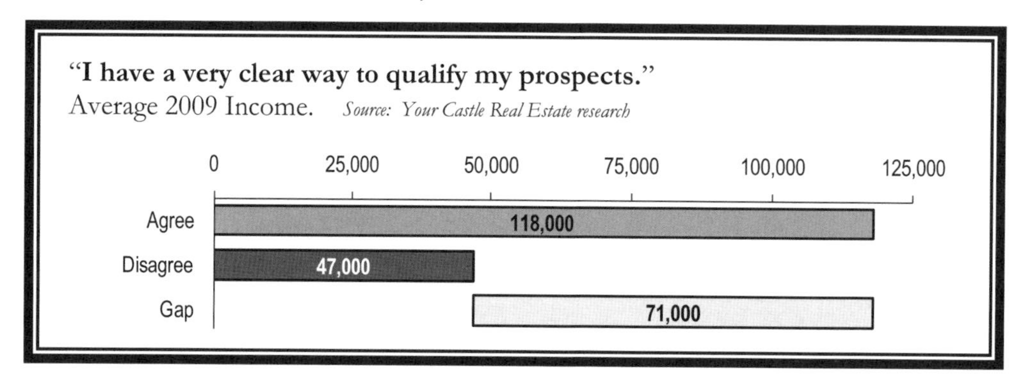

- Categories answer the questions: WHERE, HOW, WHAT and WHO. **Not WHEN.**

- **Qualifications answer the question WHEN. "WHEN do I expect this contact to convert into a client?"**

Categories are endless. However, there are only a few qualifications. Below is a simple tool to visualize the differences between categorizing and qualifying.

Categorize	Qualify
WHERE did you meet them?	WHEN will they buy or sell?
HOW do you know them?	WHEN will they buy or sell again?
WHAT do they receive from you? WHAT do they enjoy?	
WHO are they associated with?	
1. Family	1. Client A
2. Friends	Client B
3. Book Club	Blacklisted
4. Mailing List	2. Prospect A
5. Email Blast	Prospect B
6. Newsletter Recipient	Prospect C
7. Holiday Cards	Prospect X
8. Golfer	
9. Wine Connoisseur	
10. Tennis Player	
11. Service Provider	
12. Power Partner	
13. Referral Partner	

Think it through… For YOU

Take a moment to brainstorm some **CATEGORIES** that might apply to your business.

________________________ ________________________

________________________ ________________________

________________________ ________________________

________________________ ________________________

________________________ ________________________

Establishing CLEAR Database Qualifications

My clients frequently do not have a clear understanding of database qualifications. For your database to assist you in identifying where your next deal is coming from, it is essential for you to have a clear differentiation among the **QUALIFICATIONS**.

> *"I finished entering my contacts in outlook with categories and qualifications. I appreciate your training."*
>
> A salesperson that participated in the pilot efficiency classes

Think of the chart below as a ladder. This chart serves as a visual to assist you in properly defining the differences between the qualifications that I suggest you assign to your prospects and clients.

- The lowest rung on the ladder is Prospect X. This is the key factor which is frequently missing from a Sales Professionals qualification system. Prospect X is someone who you have not yet determined to be a potential client. You may have only just been referred to them. You may have not had a conversation about their needs yet.. They cannot be qualified in your database as an A, B or C Prospect until you have had a voice-to-voice or face- to-face conversation with them to inquire about their specific needs. Prospect X's will comprise your "call list"
- The highest rung on the ladder is Client A. This is the ideal qualification that you want all of your prospects to arrive at.
- Your goal is to climb the relationship ladder with your prospects until they arrive at Client A status. As you reach each rung of the ladder, this client shows you what steps to take in order to cultivate your relationships in the most proper, efficient, and affordable way.

This chart will assist you in avoiding erroneous expenditure of time and money. Many a sales professional has "invested too much" on a prospect they later discovered that was not worth the trouble. Don't let that be you. The ladder suggests the degree of time and money should be spent courting each person in your database.

To help you interpret this tool, here is a key to the symbols you will see used on the Qualification Ladder:

△ This symbol suggests your execution of The Power Triangle. Chapter 12 will explain this concept in more detail

$ This symbol indicates the degree of money you should spend on this individual. For example: The "Client A" qualification has four $$$$, while the "Prospect B" clients only have one $ indicated. This shows that the greater amount of marketing and entertaining dollars should be spent on Client A vs. Prospect B. From my experience, this example is true of most industries.

The Qualification Ladder

Qualification	Definition	Next Steps
Client A	Client. Currently sending you referrals or providing you with new opportunities. May also be a Power Partner or Referral Partner.	Entertain Client A's. Engage them in a client appreciation program. Reward for referrals. Actively refer people to them to perpetuate Netweaving effect. Market△ssively. **$$$$**
Client B ⬆	Client. Not currently sending referrals.	Teach them how to refer to you and reward them as they do. Refer to them first and provide an example of Netweaving. Market Passively **$$$**△
Prospect A ⬆	Will buy/sell quickly: in 0 – 6 months, or whatever your industry sales cycle dictates	Stay **actively** connected. Market to them **passively**. They are an A priority to your day and to your sales and marketing efforts. Netweave. **$** △
Prospect B ⬆	Will buy/sell soon; within in 7 – 12 months, or whatever your industry sales cycle dictates	Stay **actively** connected. Market to them **passively**. They are a B priority to your day and to your sale and marketing efforts. Netweave. **$**△
Prospect C ⬆	MAY buy/sell someday. Currently not interested or may have an allegiance with someone else.	Market to them **passively**. Stay connected by a thread via phone and passive marketing. **Re-qualify** quarterly or so.
Prospect X ⬆	No known qualification. Just met for the first time. Just referred to you. Meet with them and GET THEM QUALIFIED.	Follow up **within 1 day**. Set up a purposeful meeting with them within 10 days to discuss THEM. Thoughtfully orchestrate this meeting. Research them. Pre-plan what you can. INTERVIEW!

Your goals:

- Meet Prospect X's and qualify them as quickly as possible into the other rungs of the ladder.
- Elevate Prospect C's to Prospect B status, or remove them from the database if conversion looks grim.
- Migrate Prospect B's to Prospect A status.
- Close the deal. Prospect A's are now converted to Client B's
- Teach Client B's to refer business to you. They have now arrived at Client A status.

There is one additional qualification that I suggest you use. It's pretty self explanatory, and occasionally necessary. See below.

Blacklisted	Difficult to work with. You are NOT interested in any future business or any of their referrals.	Remove from all marketing campaigns and delete from marketing distribution lists. Keep in database, especially if your database sync to your phone.

How do I Manage all of the $#*!&%$ Business Cards?

If you are like most sales people, you probably have a stack of business cards. Are yours wrapped lovingly in a rubber band and sitting somewhere near your computer monitor or in a desk drawer? Go through those cards and see who is still worth following up with. If too much time has passed, the chances are slim they will be worth your time connecting. Going forward, here are some ideas so you do not lose opportunities.

> *"The Efficiency by Design 'Falling in Love with your Database' class offered me tools and lessons that I now use daily in my business. Darice Johnston gave specific examples on how to set up, organize, use and fall in love with my database. I now have over 1,500 organized clients, prospects, vendors, partners and future contacts organized with scheduled follow up connections. As Real Estate Agents, if we are not organized to follow up and continually connect with our sphere and farms, we cannot count on future business.*
>
> *I feel confident in my future business thanks to the Efficiency by Design 'Falling in Love with your Database' class in assisting me with database tools and processes I previously did not know existed."*
>
> Salesperson who participated in the pilot efficiency classes

The DOs and DON'Ts of Business Card Management

DOs:

1. Add the individual's contact information to your database and passive marketing campaign services immediately. Why? Because if you skip this step at the forefront, you immediately set the stage of lost opportunity before you have even had a chance to solidify the connection.

2. Update their qualification level in the database immediately. If you do not know when they will be ready to "buy what you are selling," then qualify them as Prospect X. With their contact information and qualification in your database, you can begin the courting process with your prospects.

3. Keep the physical business card in a business card book or plastic card sleeve in your Operations Manual (See Piles to Files, Chapter 7) until you have made a personal connection or an actual qualification with this person. Sometimes it helps to have a visual point of focus to remember who they are, how you met and what they said… especially if they have a picture or logo on their card.

4. During your pre-scheduled Happy Hour (the hour you make your phone calls), review your physical business cards and sort your database to pull up a list of your Prospect X's. Begin making calls to set appointments. Make it your intention to call each person within 24 hours of meeting them or being referred to them. Schedule an appointment within ten days of meeting that person. Does that sound difficult? Well, it is.

Most people don't do it. However, if YOU do it, your conversion rates will increase dramatically, and your income will follow.

5. Once qualified, return to your database and make notes in the customer's record. If applicable, change their qualification from Prospect X to Prospect C, B or A… and then continue your courting process appropriately to convert them from prospect to client.

6. Show consistent and genuine interest in them as a person and add value to them personally or professionally to capture their allegiance.

DON'Ts

1. Don't keep the cards on your desk wrapped in a rubber band, never to be looked at again.

2. Don't add them to your database without ALSO qualifying them as a Prospect A, B, C or X

3. Don't take someone's card assuming your will remember everything you need to about them. Write anything down you learn about them on the back of the card or input them directly into your mobile device.

4. Don't assume they do not want to hear from you. They gave you their card – which is an open invitation to reconnect.

5. Don't take someone's card if you are not going to follow up. (Ok… so I am being a bit dramatic, as social grace dictates that you always take any card offered to you. My point is that if you are not going to follow up with that person, you may as well have not taken their card. Do yourself a favor and always follow up. It is one of the highest impact ways to increase your income.

One author calls within four hours of an event – unless it is an evening event – and has experienced incredible success in doing so! If you can make your initial follow-up calls within four business hours of the event, you will see a dramatic increase in your conversion efficiency. It is much more efficient to attend fewer networking events and do a better job of following-up, than to go to many events and do a poor job of follow-up.

SOME BEST PRACTICES

If you are going to a networking event, take a moment before even attending the event to block out time in your calendar to accomplish follow up calls after the event is over. You need that blocked-out time to:

- Qualify and prioritize the leads
- Categorize the leads
- Enter the best leads into your database
- Schedule the next steps
- Execute the next steps

Personal experience has shown that follow up (usually a phone call to set up a one-on-one appointment) within 24 hours is more effective than a phone call in the second day. After the third day, conversion rates (e.g., how many calls have to make to get an appointment) drop dramatically. After the fifth day, the likelihood of you even bothering to follow up is slim. You will have forgotten about them and will be off to the races to the next networking event. Then…the cycle perpetuates.

Can you see now why there are so many lost opportunities in sales? Don't be fooled. **There is a definite correlation here. If you are not connecting into your database, you are probably not connecting into your prospects or maximizing your prospecting efforts either.**

If you get to choose when to set up or attend a networking event to meet new prospects, consider these suggestions:

- Mornings are best, as you can follow up in the afternoon.
- Monday through Thursday is best. For Thursday events, you can follow up on Friday before the weekend arrives.

Many sales people have proven that if you go to a networking event on Friday afternoon and are required to do follow up calls on Monday morning, you will be much less effective in scheduling appointments. *You do not want be "too busy." You want to be effective.*

When at the event, be sure to jot down a note or two about the person. When you sit in front of your database after the event, write down as much as you can remember. The quick note you jotted down should be enough to help you remember more details. The longer you wait between initially meeting the person and writing down these details, the less you will remember.

> *"I'm lovin' my database! My showings were cancelled this afternoon and I was so excited after our class today I jumped into my database. At first I was holding on to my old system... finally convinced myself it does not work... started over using your system and I think it really is clicking! Thanks so much..."*
>
> A salesperson who participated in the pilot efficiency classes

Business relationships have a character element (do they know you, like you and trust you?) as well as a competency element (are you good at your job?). **Your mastery of these small details proves to your prospect that you are a well-organized professional**… one with whom they should consider doing business.

Business cards and referrals are either an excellent source of business OR a huge loss of potential. **Make a decision to run your business like a business.** Be disciplined to capitalize on your leads, your referrals and honor the time you have already spent in networking and building your business.

* * * * * *

Implementation

We need to move you from having been interested to taking action. Make the commitment to improve your business.

My Commitment to My Business

- I will TAKE ACTION to make a difference in my business, TODAY!
- I stay CORE (Centered on Results Every Day).
- I EXECUTE what I am learning. I am not a perpetual student.

My greatest "AHA!" moments from this chapter were:

____

____

____

____

My 24 hour Commitment is (what idea related to this chapter can I implement in 24 hours):

____

____

____

____

My Seven Day Commitment is:

____

____

____

____

My new standard of professional excellence or habitual way of working is:

____

____

* * * * * *

What does success look like?
It's important to note that if you are doing **the majority** of the things suggested in this chapter **the majority** of the time, THAT IS SUCCESS. It's not possible to do all things, all of the time. But if you can honestly look at yourself and say that you are doing what you need to be doing about 51% of the time, that is success.

What is in the next chapter?
Do you feel like you have a handle on Database Skills? The next secret of highly efficient sales professionals is revealed in Chapter 10, "Mastering the Art of Follow-Up." This chapter will guide you through:

A. Why follow-up is essential to your income
B. How to use active campaigns to close deals
C. How to use passive campaigns to stay connected
D. Success at networking events
E. Success on the phone
F. Implementation

I would recommend investing some time this chapter if you scored a B or below on Follow-Up Skills.

10.Mastering the Art of Follow-up

The best career advice: Find out what you like doing best and get someone to pay you for doing it.
Katherine Whitehorn

Next to doing the right thing, the most important thing is to let people know you are doing the right thing.
John D. Rockefeller

How Does the "Follow-Up" Fit Into the System?
There are four Cornerstones of success. You do not necessarily need to master each of them to move on to the more advanced concepts. However, before moving on, you should be able to answer at least "neutral" instead of "disagree" on most of the Cornerstone questions on the survey in the beginning of the book.

When you have them in place, it is time to move on to Mastering the Art of Follow-Up. You will draw on the skills from each of the four Cornerstones to execute Follow-Up to its fullest potential.

This chapter will explore several essential topics:

G. Why follow-up is essential to your income
H. How to use active campaigns to close deals
I. How to use passive campaigns to stay connected
J. Success at networking events
K. Success on the phone
L. Implementation

When you finish implementing the ideas within "Follow-Up," you will be ready to put into practice Advanced Marketing Techniques, if they are of interest. If not, progress to "Action Plan" which will lead you to rapid implementation and results.

Why Follow-up is Essential to Your Income and Career Satisfaction

If you do build a great experience, customers tell each other about that. Word of mouth is very powerful.
Jeff Bezos, Founder Amazon.com

What you are about to read can make or break the escalation of your sales career. With having secured your cornerstones, you now have a solid foundation for your business. You are ready for the next level of success!

The Importance of Follow-Up

Are you good with follow-up, based on the survey at the beginning of the book (see Chapter 4)? If not, this is both good news and bad news. The good news is that you are not alone. Your struggles are the same as many others in the land of sales professionals. The BAD news is the top producer down the hall does not identify with these problems. They know ***how*** to stay connected. In addition, they ***do*** it. The gap between large and small incomes in sales is often as simple as knowing what to do and *actually getting it done*, consistently. **Top producers know how crucial follow up is. More importantly, they have the discipline to make it happen.** This chapter will show you how to implement a strong, effective system to increase communication, enhance relationships, and close more sales.

> **How Many Follow-Up Attempts Sales Professionals Make with Prospects:**
>
> - 48% of sales people never follow up
> - 25% of sales people make 1-2 contacts
> - 12% of sales people make 3 contacts
> - Only 10% of sales people make 4 or more contacts

Now that you have seen the sales statistics, you need to make a decision about your business. Where will you be in the sales statistics ladder 90 days from now? There is no need to tell me. Your income in twelve months will reflect your choices.

Relationship Sales versus Product Sales

There is a difference between relationship selling and product sales. Relationship selling is generally required when the product (and/or service) has a significantly high price point. The sales cycle is longer for these items. Alternatively, the product selling style is applicable to products or services with a small price point or a "one call close." Product sales typically have a very short sales cycle.

This chapter will address relationship selling.

Relationship selling requires you, the sales professional, to invest time, effort, energy and often a little imagination in prospecting and client retention activities. You must be engaged in your prospect's lives and businesses. Frequently, the potential client requires this rapport building before the real sales process can even begin. After a relationship has been established, the sales professional gets the opportunity to reveal their professional benefit and industry knowledge.

> **When are Sales Made?**
>
> - 2% on the first contact
> - 3% on the second contact
> - 5% on the third contact
> - 10% on the fourth contact
> - 80% on the fifth to twelfth contact

Forming New Relationships

I enjoy relationship selling. It allows me to cultivate friendships, enrich business partnerships and really make a difference in other people's lives. However, a steady stream of clients is not necessarily knocking on my company's door 24-7. I still need to get myself out into the market, gain visibility and market my company just like anyone else. Then, once I have established a handful of people interested in discussing my professional benefits further, I need to set aside time to follow up with those with whom I have connected.

Sales professionals often confront several problems in managing the sales cycle. Do you neglect to…

- Follow up with the people you just met?
- Send deliverables you promised?

- Connect your prospects to the people you told them they should meet?
- Schedule the next appointment, or clarify next steps before you end an appointment?
- Add people into your database and record memorable information about the meeting?
- Thank people for their referrals, or teach people how to refer?

Why do we neglect these things? Because we are busy racing from one appointment or event to the next. By the time the end of the day arrives, most of our momentum is lost because we have not allocated time to "follow up." As I have been counseled by my co-author Lon Welsh… "If you aren't able to schedule time after an event to follow up with the people you just met… don't bother going to the event."

For some reason, many sales professionals freeze here. Do not get me wrong. As Lon suggests, time blocking is an essential component to following up. If you have not carved out the time in your day and your week to reconnect back into the people you have met, you cannot possibly be cultivating relationships. But is that the only thing that prevents us from following up… or does it go a little deeper than that?

> *"I like my monthly newsletter and I have gotten some good feedback on it from readers. It goes out consistently and contains different types of stories, not just dry market stats."*
>
> Quote from survey

One of the reasons we have a problem following up is that we are not clear about HOW to follow up and build relationships. We do not want to be pushy or "sales-y." We want to come across as authentic and genuine. Therefore, we must answer some questions:

- How do I follow up?
- What do I say when I call?
- How do I stay connected in a purposeful and memorable way?

Having a clear plan in place can help us accomplish all of these things… even overcoming the fear of rejection.

So… what do I do next?

Every person engaged in relationship selling needs active sales techniques and passive marketing techniques. In my system I refer to the active approach as "Sales Tracks," and the passive approach as "Marketing Campaigns." Before I introduce you to the tools, let's take a look at what the survey results say about the importance of these two items.

We asked the survey respondents, "What opportunities do you have in this area?" They told us:

- "Power hours [for doing follow up calls], but I am never sure what to say, so I am constantly finding excuses for not doing them."
- "I need to spend more follow-up time with my 'A' list clients."

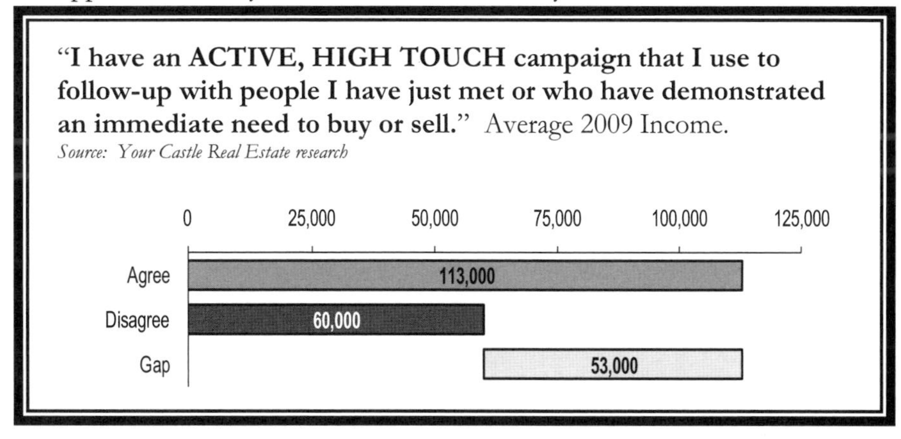

* * * * * *

What is working well for you?

- "Social Media - it is incredibly effective."
- "I send calendars, day timers, or pens (your name is always with them). I leave pens and cards (e.g., doctors' offices, grocery store). People always need pens. Keep your name in front of them."

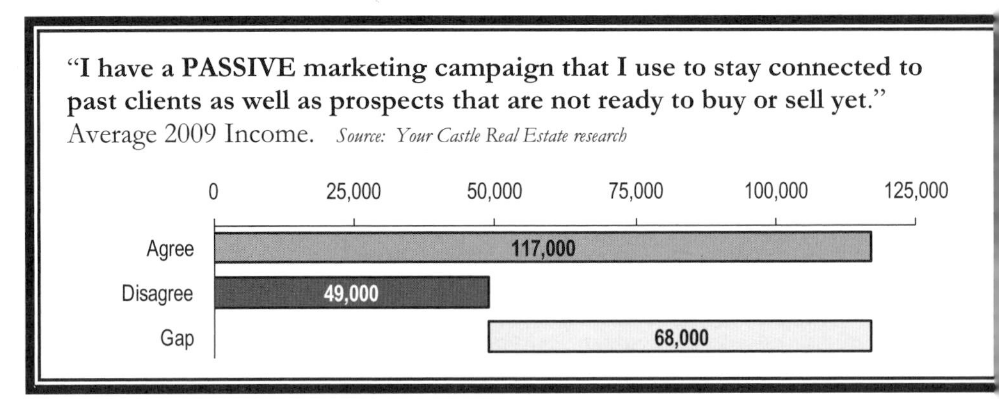

- "Calendars for fifteen years; clients ask for them. I also do quarterly mailings."

What opportunities do you have?

- "I maintain contact [with past clients], but I am always looking for relevant materials [to improve relationships]." (Income over $100K)
- "I need to find interesting information that benefits past clients who are not in the market." (Income over $100K)
- "Consistent communication; my company has a monthly email and I have only gotten a few people on the list!"
- "I pay for lots of [my database] services that I really do not put enough time into to make successful."
- "The high touch and passive marketing campaign need to be tuned up."
- "Finding a program that does not cost a lot and still be able to get in front of my clients."
- "I am not happy with my current means of passive communication with prospects. I am still looking for something that makes me stand out. Although, the fact that I keep in consistent touch with my prospects seems to be enough to set me apart from competitors."

Does this sound familiar to you? Read on for some solutions.

How to Use Active Sales Tracks to Close Your Current Prospects

Google actually relies on our users to help with our marketing. We have a very high percentage of our users who often tell others about our search engine.
Sergey Brin, co-founder, Google.

What is the difference between active and passive processes?

SALES TRACKS are *active connections*. They are specific to an individual. Sample activities include phone calls, personalized emails, personalized handwritten notes, appointments, one-on-one social media interactions and presentations. Sales Tracks are personalized, purposeful connections. They are person to person. Only the sales professional, or their assistant acting in their name, can perform these duties if they are to add real value to the relationship. They are *high effort* and *high value*, with *high pay off*.

MARKETING CAMPAIGNS are *passive connections* which are not specific to one person but reach many people within a sales professional's network. Examples include newsletters, email campaigns, mailing campaigns and one-to-many communications within social media. Many passive activities can be outsourced.

To run my business effectively, I recognized the need for these two systems. They are separate in nature but work simultaneously. These systems are in place to help me accomplish two things: to follow up and stay connected. Following up and staying connected brings me more prospects and helps me close deals.

SALES TRACKS Active Connections	MARKETING CAMPAIGNS Passive Connections
Very specific to one individual/entity Personal, purposeful "touch"	Not specific to one individual or entity Automated "touches" to your network
Sales activities include: Phone calls Emails Personalized notes Presentations Appointments 1:1 social media discussions	**Marketing activities include:** Email campaign Newsletters Mailings Using social media to share information with multiple people at the same time

Don't hide... say "Hi!"
Less effective sale people will often hide behind their marketing. "If they see my face or my name in print often enough, they will call me when they need what I am selling." WRONG! You probably have already proven this to be incorrect by having already lost a sale to your closest friends or even past clients because you did not stay verbally or physically connected. Do not be afraid to pick up that phone! Marketing serves a purpose, but it **cannot** replace personal contact. There is nothing better than the personal touch.

Sample Sales Tracks

Here is a sample Sales Track grid for one of my clients who is a real estate broker. As you can see, she developed six tracks as indicated below. She pre-designed each track to give her an idea of what she was going say on a call or what her next step was in following up. Calls should start with rapport building (family, occupation, recreation, dreams… these are great ways to get the conversation started).

As she planned these tracks out, she happened to discover some marketing tools that she realized she needed (but did not have) in order to execute this plan completely. Those items were her biography and her introduction letter. She placed an asterisk by those items so she could add them to her 90-Day Action Plan (Chapter 13 will walk you through that planning process).

Across the top of the graph below, you can see typical situations where she needs to follow up with prospects or clients. As you go down the grid, you can see the different interaction steps.

	Track 1 Just Met	**Track 2 Past Clients or Personal Sphere**	**Track 3 Open House**	**Track 4 Referred To**	**Track 5 Thank you for Referral**	**Track 6 Post Closing**
	After initial meeting:	**To re-engage or reconnect:**	**To follow-up:**	**To schedule initial meeting:**	**To express appreciation & reciprocate:**	**To stay connected & cultivate relationships:**
1	Hand Written Note	Professional or Personal Letter	Call to say thank you and qualify further	Phone Call	Phone Call	Welcome Home Gift or Service
2	Phone Call	Phone call to set up coffee	Begin sending property info	Meeting	Note with gift card	House Warming Party
3	2nd Meeting	Coffee Meeting	Send intro letter* & bio* with personal note	Hand Written Note	Meeting	Coupons for discounts on services
4	Note or Email	Hand Written Note	Meeting	Set up Power Triangle Appt	Follow-Up Email	
5	Set up Power Triangle Appt	Set up Power Triangle Appt	Hand written note	Drop into Passive Campaign	Set up Power Triangle Appt	
6	Drop into Passive Campaign	Drop into Passive Campaign	Set up Power Triangle Appt		Make sure they are in passive campaign	
7			Drop into Passive Campaign			

Personalize this graph to generate ideas for your own Sales Tracks. You can find it online at www.EfficiencyByDesign.com.

How to use Passive Campaigns to Stay Connected with Your Network

Customers do not always know what they want. The decline in coffee drinking was because most of the coffee people bought was stale and they were not enjoying it. Once they tasted ours, they found we were filling a need they did not know they had.

Howard Schultz, Chairman of Starbucks

The key words here are passive and systematized. This same client referenced above used the following form to design her Passive Marketing Campaigns. As you can see, she has a monthly, quarterly and annual campaign into which she assigns prospects and clients:

	Campaign 1 MONTHLY	Campaign 2 QUARTERLY	Campaign 3 SEMI-ANNUALLY
Who Receives?	Clients Prospects A, B	Clients Prospects A, B, C	Clients Prospects A
Jan	Seasonal Post Card	Market Statistics	Send signed and personalized New Years Letter
Feb	Seasonal Post Card		
Mar	Newsletter		Deliver Tax Time information from my CPA Partner
Apr	Seasonal Post Card	Market Statistics	
May	Seasonal Post Card		
Jun	Newsletter		Deliver seed packets or plants
Jul	Seasonal Post Card	Market Statistics	
Aug	Seasonal Post Card		
Sept	Newsletter		Coupons to Family Night restaurants
Oct	Seasonal Post Card	Market Statistics	
Nov	Seasonal Post Card		Personalized Holiday Card
Dec	Newsletter		Deliver Homemade Fudge

Personalize this chart to plan your Marketing Campaign. You can find it online at www.EfficiencyByDesignOnline.com.

My client has used her database qualifications (See Chapter 9) to determine exactly who would receive these "touches."

- She uses a company to send the post cards and newsletters, but because they cost a fair amount of money, she sends those only to her top prospects and clients.
- She automates the market share reports and sends them via email. These cost the least amount of time and money so she sends them to C Prospects, in addition to her top prospects and clients.
- She specializes in personalized touches on an annual basis. These touches cost her most time and money so they are only received by her clients and top prospects.

Now that we have gone through how to set up and organize your sales tracks and marketing campaigns, we need to connect and with new people to bring them into your business. Let's discuss some simple ways to get started on how to "reach out and touch someone" by phone and in person. We will start by discussing some face-to-face strategies.

Success at Networking Events

> *The fact is, everyone is in sales. Whatever area you work in, you do have clients and you do need to sell.*
> Jay Abraham

So… what's your line?

Picture this. You are sitting at a crowded conference table, attending a leads group for the very first time. The moderator asks everyone to introduce themselves. They get to you. What do you say to stand out?

Line One: *"Good Morning! I'm Darice Johnston, and I sell title insurance."*
Line Two: *"Good Morning! I'm Darice Johnston. I am an efficiency coach to real estate professionals."*
Line Three: *"Good Morning! I'm Darice Johnston. I help Realtors® create efficiencies in their business so they can sell more real estate."*

Tell me… which "line" has more power? I would have to say line three. While line one and two are accurate portraits of my title insurance sales career, they do not necessarily create an emotion in the people who are listening. That is why your opening line needs to adhere to this one rule: **Say what you DO, not what you ARE.**

If you want to explore this in more detail, get the book "*Make Your Contacts Count*" by Anne Baber and Lynn Waymon. It is fantastic. Here are a few more examples of saying what you DO (the value you provide) versus saying what you ARE (giving your job title)

Before	After
I am with the Association of Bicycle Professionals.	I help people connect with resources to get more bicycling into their lives. We just gave a grant to help build 300 miles of bike trails in Colorado.
I am a senior manager in the construction advisory practice of a professional services firm.	I help clients when their dream construction project turns into their worst nightmare – you know, when they are over budget or having quality issues. I just helped a client solve a dispute over the construction of a new house that was behind schedule
I'm a marketing consultant	I help people get the word out about their products and services so they can attract more customers. Last week I helped one of my clients, a CPA, get on the front page of the business section. He has had seven calls from prospective clients!

The other key insight by Baber and Waymon: The first sentence is what you do *best.* The second sentence is a *testimonial* of how you have helped a client. Get their book to get many other ideas for networking and follow-up.

Thinking Through Some Examples

Obviously, you will want to insert your industry specific ideas, below is a simple example that would be appropriate for a real estate broker:

- "I help people achieve their long-term financial goals through real estate investing."

If you wear several hats (e.g., you can provide several different types of products and services), you should ideally learn about your conversation partner first. Ask THEM questions to get to understand where they are coming from. Then, when they reciprocate and ask what *you* do, you can give them a response that is more likely to tie to their needs. For example:

- **Investment Realtor:** "I help people find investment properties with great cash flow that are easy to manage. I just helped a client buy a rental condo. It has $400 per month of positive cash flow, even with a property manager answering all of the tenant's questions!"

- **Retail Realtor:** "I help families find homes that are a perfect fit for their busy lives and put their kids in great schools. I just used my firm's custom software to help a client buy a home that was $30,000 under market that was in one of the best school districts."

- **Managing Broker:** "I help Realtors get to the next level of their career. An agent that joined me from Acme Realty last year has seen his production increase 30% in a down market with our specialized tools and training."

What is your new opening line?

____

____

What is the testimonial that you will share after you share your opening line?

____

____

What other opening lines might you use in certain situations?

____

____

Success on the Phone

> *A market is never saturated with a good product, but it is very quickly saturated with a bad one.*
> Henry Ford

What do I say after I say "Hello?"
Sales Professionals, I would like to introduce you to your new best friend, the telephone.

> *"I mail to past clients twice each month and receive thank you notes from them for the items that I send."*
>
> Quote from survey

How often have you avoided picking up the phone because you do not know what to say, or what approach to take? In this section of this chapter, let's address the REAL REASON you need to pick up that phone. If you are wondering, "What do I say after I say, Hello?" here is a good rule of thumb is to remember: "Focus on the means, NOT the end"

THE END is the close. The Sale. THE MEANS are all of the things you do to get to THE END. While THE END may be your real objective, what do you think is most meaningful to your client? The answer is, "THE MEANS." Here are a few objectives for you to remember while using the telephone to begin building relationships:

The Telephone is The MEANS to THE END. Use it to:

- Follow-up with people you have just met
- Set appointments
- Communicate information
- Strengthen relationships
- Add a personal touch to frequently impersonal processes
- Qualify the probability of a potential relationship… client, business partner or referral partner

No one wants to be sold… but people sure do love to buy. For products with a longer sales cycle, the key is to remember that people want to buy from people they like, or with whom they have a relationship. As a sales professional on commission, it may be hard to not focus on "the end" because that is *your* main objective. However, your potential client is more interested in the means… and they will be able to tell if you aren't. It is a huge turn off for most buyers. To turn your focus away from the end, focus on these ideas:

- Get to know them better.
- Discover how you can be of help to them personally or professionally.
- Identify who you can connect them to in your sphere of influence to initiate a Power Triangle (see Chapter 12)
- Aim to qualify them as a potential referral partner/business partner now and worry about qualifying them as a client later.

As you will learn in The Power Triangle chapter, you are NOT out there just looking for clients. You are looking for Business Partners, Affiliate Partners and Referral Partners as well. These individuals are JUST AS IMPORTANT to secure as capturing a client. Here is a great script to use when you pick up the phone to call a prospect to show that you focus on THE MEANS:

> *"Hi Michael, This is Darice Johnston. It was great to meet you last night at _________. I would love to get to know a little bit more about:*
>
> - You and your profession
> - The project you are working on
> - The initiative you mentioned
> - The person you referenced/referred
>
> *"Because of my profession, I am pretty well connected, and what you said really sparked my interest. I was hoping to schedule a coffee appointment with you in the next few days."*

"Darice, if I am not focusing on 'the end', at what point do I let them know what I do?"
Imagine you are connecting with a potential client over a cup of coffee, inquiring about their life, their work, their products and services. At some point in the conversation, they are either bound to ask you about what you do or you will find a few opportunities at which to interject this information. At that point, use your "new opening line" and elaborate as appropriate. Let them know how you are different from your competition by conveying your Differentiating Point (see Chapter 11). Then let them know the kind of client you work with, in case they have anyone in their sphere that may benefit from your services.

Who knows… that person may be them.

When it comes to the telephone… intention is KEY:
Have you ever picked up a ringing phone only to find the person on the other end of the line requesting answers to questions you were not prepared to answer? You may have felt flustered by the call, obligated to answer or pressured to respond. The reason this occurred is that YOU did not initiate the call. The CALLER knew what THEIR intention was, but as the person on the receiving end, you were obliged to flow along with THEIR intention.

Had you taken a moment to ask them to hold, you could gather your thoughts about what you want to accomplish with this caller and you could have eliminated the flustered feelings. When you receive a call, don't be afraid to take a moment to ask them to hold. Then ask yourself the question, "What is MY real intention with this call?" You may want to:

- Be heard.
- Be understood.
- Understand the other party.
- Show real value of your product.
- Be present for the conversation.

Then you could get back on the call and feel more comfortable, confident and prepared to *respond* to their questions rather than *react* to them.

You can use this same concept when you place the call. Before placing a call to a prospect, ask yourself the same questions as above. "What is my real intention with this call? What outcome do I want?"

- I want to be friendly.
- I want to understand and be understood.
- I want to convey the real value of my product.
- I want to put my prospect at ease.
- I want to set an appointment.
- I want to get a commitment.

Know what your intention is and have an idea of what you would like to say before you pick up the phone. If you have a clear understanding of why you are calling and a clear intention of what you are attempting to accomplish, you will deliver your message in a much more professional, less "canned" way.

Create Great Reasons to Call:
Sales professionals often make the sales call impersonal. Yes, your clients and prospects need what you have to sell. Yes, you want to communicate that value to them frequently. However, they would also love to know you are interested and engaged in other facets of life. Social Media has proven that people want to know about other peoples' lives. Try calling for reasons other than business. Alternatively, initiate the discussion with a few non-business topics to build rapport before diving into business.

Just for an experiment, place a call for no other purpose other then to be in contact. Let them know they crossed your mind. Have no further agenda. See what happens, and where the conversation goes. You may be surprised!

Phone Scripts & Conversation Points

Reconnecting with Past Clients
If you have not made the time to call your past clients for a while, reconnecting after too much time has passed can be uncomfortable. Do not use that as an excuse to avoid the phone! Here are a few ideas (reasons) for connecting:

- Give them newsworthy information related to them personally or professionally.
- Ask them about their career or their family. Leverage whatever you have an awareness of in their life to cultivate a deeper connection.
- Discover how you can bring benefit to them financially or emotionally through new connections (e.g., Power Triangles, see Chapter 12)
- Identify who you can connect them to in your sphere of influence.

Here are a few good scripts to use in order to get the phone call rolling:

Industry Related Script

"Jon, you know that I rarely pick up the phone to connect with you about _______________, but I need to let you know about a conference I recently attended concerning the economy. I have information I am sure you would want to know about. Do you have a few minutes for me?"

Power Triangle Script

"I was just introduced to someone I think you should meet who may make a real difference in your (business/life). I would love to connect you with them – maybe we can all meet for coffee next week?"

"Thinking of You" Script

"It has been an absolute shame how much time has passed since we have connected last! I would really love to catch up and see how you and your family are doing."

The Invitation - CREATE a great reason to call!

- You will be attending an event and would love to include them.
- You heard about a great community event and you wanted to make them aware of it.
- You will be hosting an event that benefits the community and you want them to know about it.
- You are hosting a client appreciation program to honor them and their allegiance to you.
- You are holding a happy hour to help them network with some key people who can benefit them in their business.

Basic Phone Etiquette

If you have picked up the phone and made the call, one of two things will happen. Your will get them live, or you will be directed into their voicemail.

If they answer:

- Introduce yourself by first and last name. I cannot tell you how many people named "Judy" I know. How many times have you had to fake the conversation until you can figure out which "Judy" it is?
- Use your company name, when appropriate.
- BE SURE to ask, "Have I caught you at a good time?" If they say no, offer to call back. Ask what time would be more convenient for them. Make SURE you call them back in a timely fashion.
- Begin the conversation on a personal note as often as you can, "First of all, how are you?" Reference something personal from the last time you saw them or connected.

If you get voice mail:

- Do not hang up. In these days of "Caller ID," they will know that you called, anyway.
- Use your full name, especially if your name is common.
- Leave your phone number at the beginning and end of the message just in case the phone connection is bad.

- Less is more! Do not give too much information unless you really have to. Your objective is to connect.
- SLOW DOWN. Do not speak too quickly, especially while giving phone numbers.
- Use single numbers : 303-555-1234, not 303-555- "twelve" "thirty-four"
- DO NOT use "words" in your phone numbers without also giving the numbers directly. "Word" phone numbers were fun BB (Before BlackBerry), but those days are long gone. Most BlackBerry users do not know how to use that feature of their phone so "word" phone numbers are very frustrating.
- Try to call from the number at which you want to receive calls. If you want them to call you on your cell phone, call them from your cell phone, not another number. Then they can just hit "8" (on most voicemail systems) to return the call. This increases the odds they will call back. Many people return calls while they are driving, so by doing this one thing, you are adding a level of convenience to this person's day.

Here is a great voice mail script:

- "Hi, ___________this is _______ ___________. 303-555-1212
- I have a very quick question for you regarding _________________________(or) I have some important news for you regarding ___________________________
- I wanted to connect with you when you have the time - no rush – and would love to hear back when you have about 3-5 minutes. Again, my number is 303-555-1212.

* * * * * *

Implementation

Wasn't that interesting to read? But now we need to move you from having been interested to <u>taking action</u>. Make the commitment to improve your business.

My Commitment to My Business

☐ I will TAKE ACTION to make a difference in my business, TODAY!
☐ I stay C.O.R.E. (Centered on Results Every Day).
☐ I EXECUTE what I am learning. I am not a perpetual student.

My greatest "AHA!" moments from this chapter were:

____

____

____

____

My 24-hour Commitment is (what idea related to this chapter can I implement in 24 hours):

____

____

____

____

My Seven Day Commitment is:

____

____

____

____

My new standard of professional excellence or habitual way of working is:

____

____

____

____

* * * * * *

What does success look like?
It's important to note that if you are doing **the majority** of the things suggested in this chapter **the majority** of the time, THAT IS SUCCESS. It is not possible to do all things, all of the time. However, if you can honestly look at yourself and say that you are doing what you need to be doing about 51% of the time, that is success.

What is in the next chapter?
If you have completed this chapter, that means your self-assessment on each of your Cornerstone skills is at a "B" level or higher. You have the basics down pretty well. You may now have a list of things to implement from this chapter on Follow-Up. If uncovered many ideas here to implement, I would suggest you focus on those first. Then proceed to the Advanced Marketing ideas in Chapters 11 and 12.

If you feel you have Follow-Up running as well as your Cornerstones, then skim Chapter 11 and 12 and see which one you might want to implement first. Chapter 11 reveals the next secret of highly efficient sales professionals, "Positioning Yourself Uniquely." This chapter will guide you through:

A. Identifying your real value
B. Discovering your Differentiating Point
C. Stepping into the role you are longing to play
D. Learning the process of creation
E. Implementation

11. Positioning Yourself Uniquely

Learning from mistakes and constantly improving products is a key in all successful companies. Listening to customers is a big part of that effort. You have to study what customers say about their problems with your products and stay tuned into what they want, extrapolating from leading-edge buyers to predict future requirements.
Bill Gates

How Does "Positioning Yourself Uniquely" Fit Into the System?
There are four Cornerstones of success. You do not necessarily need to master each of them to move on to the more advanced concepts. However, you should be able to answer at least "neutral" instead of "disagree" on most of the Cornerstone questions on the survey in the beginning of the book. After strengthening your Cornerstones, you must get your Follow-Up systems in place and functioning. Once you feel you have a good handle on Follow-Up, you can consider implementing the Advanced Marketing techniques. You will need to draw on the skills from each of the four Cornerstones and Follow-Up if you want to implement the Advanced Marketing systems to their fullest potential. This is where the rubber really meets the road!

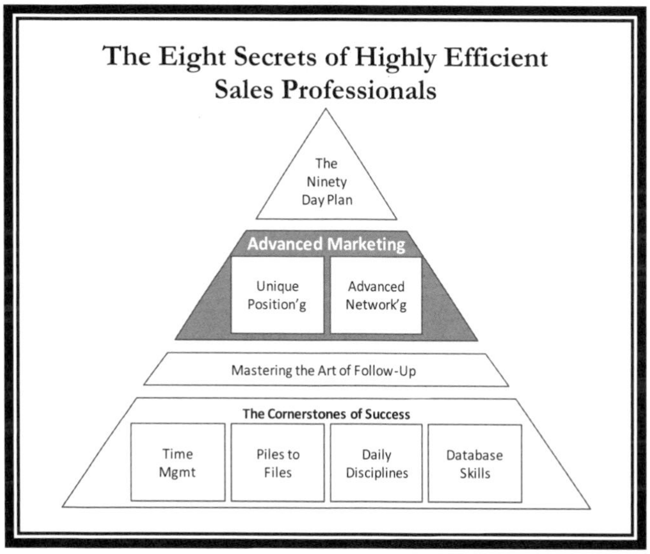

The Eight Secrets of Highly Efficient Sales Professionals

The Ninety Day Plan
Advanced Marketing
Unique Position'g
Advanced Network'g
Mastering the Art of Follow-Up
The Cornerstones of Success
Time Mgmt
Piles to Files
Daily Disciplines
Database Skills

This chapter will explore several essential topics:

A. Identifying "Your" Value
B. Methods of Differentiation
C. Discovering Your Differentiating Point
D. Case Study
E. Using Service Level as a Differentiating Point
F. Stepping into Your Role
G. Implementation

When you finish implementing the ideas within this chapter, progress to the final chapter, "The Ninety-Day Action Plan." It will guide you to rapid implementation and results.

My goal in this chapter is to give you new ideas for making yourself memorable and more valuable to your clients without give-away items or substantial extra cost. I refer to this new idea as your Differentiating Point. When you are clear about your Differentiating Point, (what makes you unique and different within your industry) you will deliver a higher degree of value than you ever thought possible. Remember:

Money is simply a measurement of the DEGREE OF VALUE you have provided in your market place.

Does establishing ourselves uniquely apart from our competitors really matter? Yes! Our survey of sales professionals show that the people who have mastered this concept make **more than twice as much money** as those who have not.

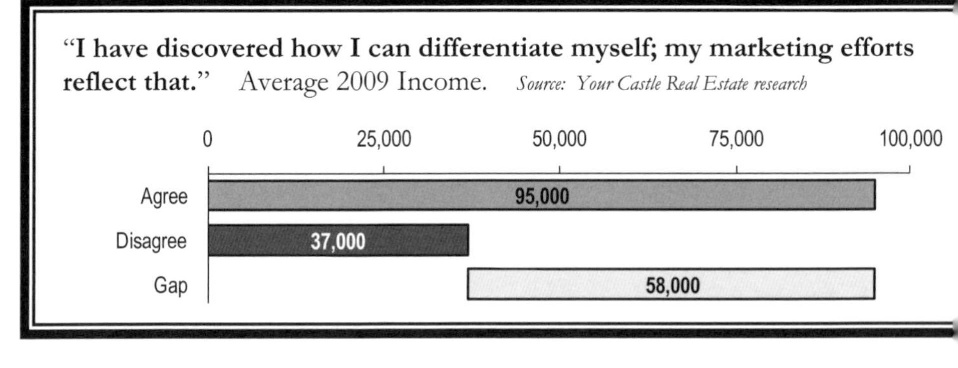

On the survey, we asked, "What is working well for you for differentiation?"

- "Through my volunteer activities, I make sure my name and business name are included on websites and in print publications."
- "I send a high value mailing. It is very popular."
- "One word - consistency. Just pick something and do it."
- "I stay in touch with vendors so I can help grow their business and they can help mine."
- "Putting my feet on the street!"
- "Talk with everyone with whom I come in contact and listen for needs. Make it known what I do."

We also asked, "What opportunities do you have?"

- "I need to increase my technical skills; especially with effective social media networking." (Income over $100K)
- "I need to join more local groups, clubs and be more visible socially."
- "I work with seniors as about 45% of my business and they do not require as much computer attention. It is almost all in person. I could expand my web skills. I do not blog and probably should."
- "Coordinate technology, print, and direct mail in a strategic and intentional way."
- "Figuring out the best way to 'touch' individual clients. Everyone responds to different 'touches'."

Identifying "Your" Value

No matter how many "items of value" you give away, the real value you bring to the table is YOU. You will be substantially more memorable if you create a unique set of qualities that only you can provide. Often that uniqueness has to do with you as a person. It can also have to do with the people that you know and the value they can bring to your clients. (We will delve into this further in Chapter 12, Networking and The Power Triangle).

Value and Your Differentiating Point

Your unique value, as **perceived by the client**, is linked to your Differentiating Point. When going through the process of discovering your Differentiating Point, remember:

- You become more valuable when you have a Differentiating Point.
- To stand out in your industry, you have to become uniquely outstanding.
- Your value has to become an essential need of your clients.
- Your Differentiating Point is a powerful money attractor because of the positive feelings you emanate when you are living and working from a place of passion and excitement.

If you do not have a point of differentiation, then you are a **commodity.** A commodity is a service or product that is so similar to its competitors that the client can trade out for another provider and not notice much of a difference. If there are no features or benefits you can use to attract clients, then the basis of competition is **price**. Do you want clients to select you because you provide the service cheaper than everyone else does? Or do want to provide something extra – that is valued by clients – for which they will pay a premium? Ideally, they will pay a premium for your unique feature and they will go out of their way to buy it from you. When you achieve this, you have developed a powerful Differentiating Point.

Most service providers – banks, cell phone providers, insurance agents, mortgage brokers, real estate agents – say they provide better service than anyone else. Even if they DO provide superior service, it is difficult for the consumer to see this while they are deciding which service provider to hire. Self-serving statements are usually ignored by consumers. Think about it. Do you believe your bank when they say:

- "We provide the best service"
- "We are number one at X"
- "We have the best products available on the market today."

I don't.... because every other company is saying it the same thing! So, challenge yourself as you read this chapter to think of a Differentiating Point that consumers will readily accept. Here is an example. A top Canadian Realtor, Craig Proctor, used to give his clients a guarantee: "If I do not sell your home in ninety days, I will buy it." Do you think that set him apart from his competitors? Did it ever! In his sales training classes, Proctor says: "If you tell your client what is unique about you, and they say 'Wow, how do you do that?'... you have it nailed." He sells over 600 homes a year and is in the top ten for Re/Max globally.

A good way to start the process of selecting a Differentiating Point is to see what research exists about consumer behavior for your industry. For example, the National Association of Realtors (a trade association) does an annual survey of consumers. They ask many questions about the consumer's purchase or sale of a home. One of the questions on the survey is, "Why did you select the Realtor that you hired?" This type of information can provide you with insights. See if your trade association does similar research studies.

There are many ways for you to add value to your clients. One of them is to pursue additional training or designations within your industry. This knowledge helps you develop solutions that are more valuable for your clients. Our survey findings are proof positive that designations contribute momentarily to establishing your importance of The Differentiating Point:

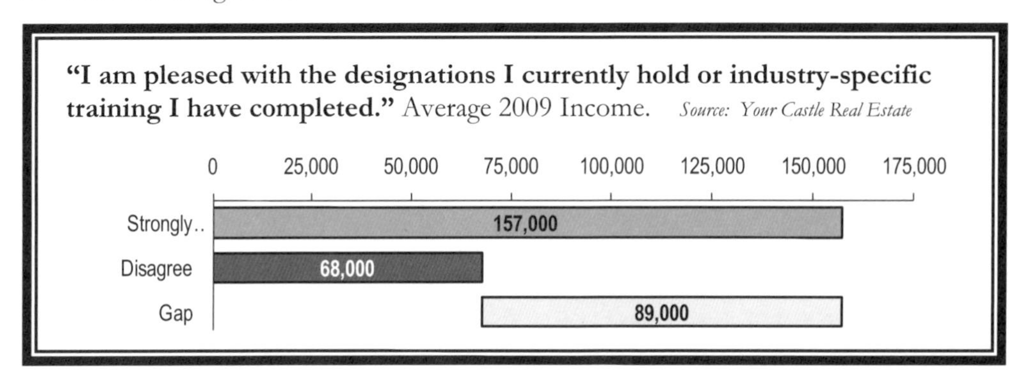

Another example of how you can add value to your clients, and set yourself apart from your competition, is market knowledge. This played a substantial role in the income differences between low producers and top producers as revealed by our survey:

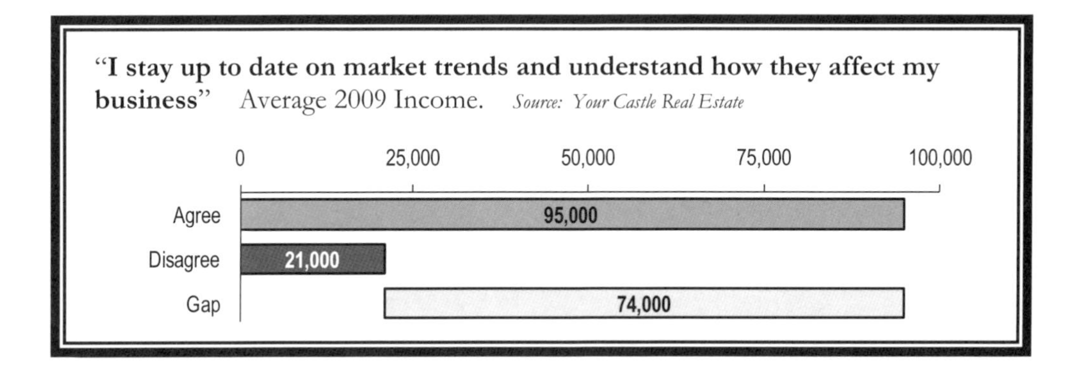

Methods of Differentiation

Your unique differentiation will probably be one (or a combination) of the following:

1. Deepening relationships in a way that cannot be replicated.
2. Developing a "value-add" that eliminates the competition.
3. Your personal identity and passionate interests.

Let's examine each of these more closely.

Deepening relationships in a way that cannot be replicated.

What helps people helps business.
Leo Burnett

Allow me to introduce my co-author Bruce Gardner. He is a full time coach and mentor at Your Castle Real Estate. He helps agents develop their differentiation strategy. He developed the next few pages to start you thinking about how you can break free from the competition by creating deeper, more meaningful relationships.

Creating deep and meaningful relationships are a proven method for developing a Differentiating Point. It may make you impervious to the efforts of your competitors. Sales people who understand this concept seek to know as much as possible about their customers and clients. We will explore a few examples:

A. Interests and hobbies
B. Collegiate loyalties
C. Family details
D. Items of value

By engaging your clients and prospective clients on this level, you can transcend the typical salesperson-customer relationship. Your customers and clients see you as business partner and a friend, someone with whom they would be comfortable socializing with or entertaining on a personal level. In many cases, the relationship comes first and the business dealings are secondary.

A. Interests and Hobbies.

Your customers and clients have interests outside of their business roles, and you can benefit from learning about these interests. They may be interested in boating, for example. You can improve your relationship with them by knowing and leveraging this information. What would the impact be if you…

- Introduced your client to a competitive boat racer?
- Gave them tickets to a competitive boating event?
- Introduced them to a principle owner of a local boat dealership?

Would any of these ideas improve your relationship with this client? Would these help make you top-of-mind? Absolutely.

Another idea would be to email this client pertinent and interesting articles about their interest or hobby. A little of this could go a long way. The message you send by doing this is that you care, you listen and that you remembered something that was important to them. It is easily accomplished by engaging a web-based news alert system like Google News. With this kind of free service, you can select the applicable article criteria, then receive notice of published articles via email that you can be send off to your client.

If your client is an avid golfer and is making a trip to a location near a storied course, how would they feel if you set them up with a tee time? Or even connected them to a member of that club who can welcome them on their visit? Would this result in a higher value relationship between you and your client? I am certain of it.

By asking about your clients' interests and/or hobbies and making note of them, you will be positioned to grow the relationship beyond a simple business interaction. When you talk with this client, you can bring up this topic and ask about it. That alone will benefit you. If you remember nothing else from this chapter, never forget the following:

"Focus on the relationship first, and then business will follow." Chinese Proverb

B. Collegiate Loyalties.

Many of your clients may have attended a college during their education that still holds a special place in their hearts. This may present another opportunity to grow your relationship.

What if you could connect them with other local graduates from this same college? You may have these people already within your network. By asking about schools attended in normal conversation and then connecting these people together, you have brought something into their lives that your competition did not. When you have benefitted someone in this way, they naturally want to reciprocate. The easiest way for them to do that is by doing business with you or referring business to you. It is a win-win.

C. Family Details.

This is another powerful way to grow your relationships: ask about families and family members. Knowing that your client's daughter was recently in a big swim meet and taking the time to ask about it can open up entirely new levels of your relationship. Again, it shows that you care and that you listen. Knowing that one of your clients' children is moving on to a university and finding a way to assist the child with the transition by way of an introduction builds a solid relationship with your clients. Knowing that your client's wife has a small business and proactively sending her some customers could make a big impact. Be imaginative! These ideas can greatly benefit your clients outside of the realm of the product and service you sell. They are sure to improve the value of your relationships with them.

D. Giving Items of Value.

In many industries, it is customary to give away marketing items to your client base to remind them of your company and its products. The items will vary by industry, but the concept is the same and the practice is very common. When you add to the effort by giving your clients other items of value (appropriate to their personal interests), you take the relationship to a new level. Be creative. Tap into your knowledge of them on a personal level and connect in a meaningful way. The cost of the item or gift need not be very high to deliver a significant impact. You are seen as someone who genuinely listens and cares… and those qualities seem to be in short supply in today's world.

Which differentiation method(s) can you use that might be well received by your clients?

____

____

____

Learn about your clients' interests, their families and their lives so you can establish deeper relationships that pay dividends for both of you.

Developing a "Value-Add" That Eliminates the Competition.

Don't focus on making a million dollars. Focus on providing a million dollars worth of service.
James Arthur Ray

Your competitors may have similar products at similar prices. They may all claim "excellent service," just like you do. How then do you eliminate the competition in such an environment? The answer may be to develop some way of delivering additional value that your competitors cannot replicate. It may help you become irreplaceable and help keep your competition at a distance. Create an additional benefit that your clients enjoy and you can be in a class of your own. This can be your Differentiating Point.

Industry Specific Value-Add's. Your industry is probably unique in many ways, so how do you create a powerful value add? What could help you become unique? Here are some ideas:

- Get an advanced industry designation for a higher level of competence.
- Add another degree that compliments your existing credentials. This may help you understand your client's needs on a broader level, and develop solutions to multi-level problems.
- Build a network of other professionals from complimentary industries that can be consulted for specific situations that may relate to your customers' needs.
- Develop a consultative skill set that helps your clients do their jobs better.

Ask yourself these questions to develop a Value-Add. Your answers may open up some opportunities currently hidden to you:

- What are some of the typical challenges faced by your clients in their industry, and how can you be instrumental in helping solve them?
- Research your client's competitors and analyze how your client might develop a competitive advantage in their marketplace.
- What do similar industries do to create a competitive advantage? Can some of those ideas be adapted to your client's situation?
- What economic or market trends are affecting your client's business and what would help them overcome the resulting challenges?

Your goal is to find a significant method of delivering additional value to your clients that cannot be easily replicated by your competitors. The answer may be industry specific, it may be a complimentary skill or talent that you possess that benefits them, or it may be an idea from another industry. Ask yourself what might be an added benefit for your clients, and seek a way to deliver this benefit to them *through you.*

Which unique value-add could you provide to your clients?

____

____

____

Your Personal Identity and Passionate Interests.

This segment is about what makes you uniquely you, and how that might impact your business relationships. Sharing this with your clients can be a terrific way to build a remarkable connection with them.

- What makes you unique as a person?
- Do you have hobbies and interests that might interest your clients?
- Do you have a charitable interest or an interest in a specific non-profit endeavor?
- Do you have a passion for helping those less fortunate or in need?
- Do you participate in a group recreational activity that you could invite your clients to partake in?
- Do you have some other non-business element in your life that you could incorporate into your business identity?

These questions may lead you to consider a new approach that is memorable for your clients. It may make you completely unique and appealing in their eyes and become your Differentiating Point. We will help you explore this is more detail in the exercise at the end of this chapter.

Case Study

So far, this all probably sounds pretty interesting, but slightly abstract. To illustrate the power of a strong Differentiating Point, let's use a real-life case study: Laura Cowperthwaite, a Realtor that founded the Thriving Artist Alliance. Here is the impact on her life, in her words:

> *I entered the real estate business in 2005 as a single mother of three boys, just as the market was preparing to take a dive. My first two years were crazy. I had an exponential learning curve and no focus to my business. I chased every possible lead that came my way and took every class I could. I tried to apply a dozen lead generation activities, all while attempting to create my systems and build a database. As my mother would say, "I was busier than a one armed paperhanger with a two legged stool." I closed one deal my first year on an $110,000 condo. At the end of my first year, I was enthusiastic and completely exhausted. I had some systems in place, had a good start on my database and had one member of my team in place (my home inspector).*
>
> *In the middle of my second year, I hired a business coach. I thought if I had someone to cheer me on and hold me accountable, I could turn 3 deals into 30. This first coach espoused 20 calls a day to FSBOs [homes for sale by owner] & expired [listings] or wherever else I could get phone numbers. This approach made me miserable and I was seriously considering leaving the business. Then 8 months into the 12-month coaching contract I was $5,000 poorer and had closed only 6 deals. This was not enough to support my boys. At the*

end of my second year, I was seriously considering leaving real estate and getting a J.O.B. Then I met two people who helped me change everything.

I met a new coach, Bruce Gardner, and I began working with a new lender, Matt Hanson (the first of conservatively more than a dozen who genuinely cared about my business). Both Bruce and Matt asked key questions that I had not thought to ask let alone try to answer.

Bruce's question: "If you could work with any type of client you wanted who would that person be?" Matt's question: "Where do you see yourself in 5-10 years?" Each question was powerful on its own but together they flipped a switch in my mind and more importantly in my heart. My answers: my ideal client is creative, an artist. My passion since early childhood has been theatre, film, music, and the arts. Prior to real estate, I had acted, directed, produced, and promoted creative endeavors of all kinds. Creative people were the people I most wanted to be around. My 5-10 year vision is to be a leader in the creative community both in terms of philanthropy and in making real and positive contributions to the quality of life lead by the creative person. I had given up this dream because earning a living took precedence. It had not dawned on me that I could do both.

Matt and Bruce's questions brought my passions and my livelihood into alignment and gave birth to my real estate team, Thriving Artist Alliance [TAA]. *Now when asked what I do, I answer "I help creative people build wealth through real estate."*

This new focus to my business has not been without its challenges and pit falls. The difference now is that the normal twists, turns and set backs are simply opportunities to refine my methods of providing meaningful value and services for my clients. Bringing my business and passions into alignment has resolved all those nagging disconnected elements in my life and my business. Now the financial contributions I make to art organizations are also a business expense. I get to support organizations I care about and the organization receives cash to support their endeavors. Anytime I attend the theatre, go to a gallery opening or see a new band play, I am doing something I love… and I am networking. When staying in touch with my network, we talk about art and ideas, their latest event or what project they are currently working on. Occasionally real estate comes up but only they introduce the subject. No more do I put off making my FORD [Family, Occupation, Recreation, Dreams] relationship calls because I do not know what to say. Now I simply stay in touch with the people I love.

The creative community is like a close-knit family. Artists are unique in how they approach their world. This has led to a variety of new methods for marketing – all integrated and directed by my unique value proposition. Everyone who works on the TAA team is an artist: Tracy an actress/playwright, Lil a vocalist with a rock band, Matt a writer. Together we have sharpened the focus of our lead generation and relationship building activities.

Strategic Partners: trade organizations and professional groups who help us reach their membership. Example partners include Denver Office of Cultural Affairs, Colorado Theatre Guild, Scientific and Cultural Facilities District, & the various arts districts.

Speaking Engagements: we speak of the economic power of the creative spirit and the role creative businesses play in the growing Colorado economy. We discuss the unique relationship between Creatives and real estate and how our listeners can leverage that relationship to improve their financial well-being.

Internet: www.thrivingartistalliance.com: a powerful tool and gathering place designed to engage, educate and empower Creatives in their art and their lives. Members can access financial and real estate information and tools, search the MLS, post their art and events, network with others. We also use Social Networking on Facebook and Twitter.

Event Attendance & Sponsorship: TAA is a corporate sponsor of Curious Theatre; we sponsor cocktail mixers & other social gatherings for creative organizations. Some other elements of my Differentiating Point:

- *Monthly Arts Calendar mailing*
- *Lender, Matt Hanson, knows how to get loans done for 1099 employees. A very important element as most creative people are independent workers who have income from a variety of sources.*
- *When helping an artist sell their home we encourage them to hang their art on the walls with price cards just as they would in a gallery.*
- *TAA photographers provide the cover photography on YCRE Trends booklets.*
- *"Creative People" postcards promoting the special talents of our clients.*

Once my passions and my real estate business came into alignment, the chaos in my life evaporated. Every time I face a business choice the strength and clarity of my Differentiating Point shows me the right way. The better I get at communicating my unique value proposition, the more my phone rings. There is, in my view, no more powerful choice an agent came make about their business than defining their Differentiating Point. Once you do, everything else falls into place.

This example shows how Laura created a powerful Differentiating Point. Do you think that Bruce and Matt also set themselves apart from their competition? Have they become *irreplaceable?* Absolutely. This is how powerful discovering and living your Differentiating Point can really be.

Discovering Your Differentiating Point

Progress is measured by the degree of differentiation within a society.
Herbert Read

Give yourself time to consider the following questions. I am confident you will conclude this exercise with greater clarity of your unique value offering which will make a substantial impact in your business.

1. What am I passionate about, in life and in business?

____

____

____

2. What was my career before this sales position?

3. What clubs and associations am I currently involved in or have been involved with?

4. What life values do I deem to be most important?

5. What activities do I most enjoy?

6. What similar qualities and interests exist in the people who I enjoy being around?

7. What drives me and motivates me?

____

8. What are my personal hobbies and interests?

9. What adds meaning to my life?

10. What is the one message I would shout from the rooftops if I knew everyone was listening… and no one would judge me for saying it?

11. What past experiences have I had that were life-changing?

Now that you have taken the time to think through what makes you unique and stand out, it is time to find ways of living your Differentiating Point and incorporating it into your sales business. **Putting My Differentiating Point Into Action.**

12. How is my Differentiating Point valuable to others?

____

____

____

13. To whom, specifically, is it valuable?

____

____

____

14. Who can support the message and delivery of my value?

____

____

____

15. How can I conduct my business in a way that reflects my Differentiating Point?

____

____

____

16. How does my Differentiating Point give me a powerful advantage?

____

____

____

17. What activities, groups, clubs, programs, non-profit organizations, etc. will I participate in to best support and express my Differentiating Point?

____

____

____

18. What marketing efforts will I create to best support and express my Differentiating Point?

____

____

____

19. What industries would appreciate and work well with my Differentiating Point?

____

____

____

20. What Power Partners can I leverage to further spotlight or strengthen my business and marketing efforts now that I have defined my Differentiating Point?

____

____

____

21. Who in my database would be a Power Partner to best support the expression of my Differentiating Point?

____

____

____

22. What unique and out-of-the-box thing(s) can I do to express my Differentiating Point?

____

____

____

23. What media options and venues are available to me to express my Differentiating Point? (e.g., Meet-up groups, blogs, web pages, social media, newspaper columns, radio shows, public television.)

____

____

____

24. How should I change my branding to be more powerful and more reflective of my Differentiating Point?

____

____

____

25. How is my Differentiating Point newsworthy? Who do I think would interview me to share what I am doing with my community and targeted audience?

____

____

____

26. How can I leverage what I just uncovered into my Sales Career? Where is the angle?

____

____

____

You may need assistance with this last question. Attend one of my classes or contact me personally. My team and I are excited to help you incorporate your discoveries into developing your Differentiating Point.

Using Service Level as a Differentiating Point

Customers buy for their reasons, not yours.
Orvel Ray Wilson

Imagine an upscale environment – shopping at Nordstrom's, dinner at The Ritz. As a sales professional and business owner, you can create a similar feeling and experience for each of your clients, appropriate to your industry, regardless of the cost of your products or services.

> *"I have acquired most of my clients just through being active in other aspects of life: Recreation, volunteering, classes, etc."*
>
> Survey Respondent

Now let's talk about "mediocrity." Webster's defines mediocre as "of a middle quality; of a moderate or low degree of excellence; indifferent; ordinary." Take an honest look at your own business. Does the word "indifferent" describe you, the level at which you engage with your clients, your response time to inquiries, your staff or your service level? Is any element of your business mediocre? Here are some simple ways that you can create an exceptional service experience – no matter what your industry or audience may be:

- Set the example and if possible train your staff to engage with each patron. Eye contact is important, as is thoroughness of completing orders or providing services.
- Train your staff to create familiarity with clientele. Use first names when possible, or Mr./Mrs. if appropriate.
- Anticipate your client's needs before they mention they have them.
- Keep yourself, your car and your office environment attractive, inviting, organized and clean.
- Do something to WOW your customers. Depending upon your industry, there may be some regulations limiting what you can do… but I guarantee you that creating an exceptional service experience will never be one of them.
- Always thank people for their business.
- Stay close to and connected with your top clients. Do more for them then just providing your products and services. Use the concept of The Power Triangle (see Chapter 12) to help them build their business and make a difference in their lives.
- Give rewards or small gifts for referrals…or at the very least, send a hand-written thank you notes to the clients who refer others to you.

Do not focus on making a million dollars. Instead, focus on giving a million dollars worth of service. As you live your Differentiating Point and create exceptional service experiences for your customers, you will quickly attract new clientele. Your rewards… both financial and relational… will be abundant.

> *"On Thursday after that class, I called the Association of Bridal Consultants to see if they'd be interested in having me talk to them at their next meeting. Turns out, it was Thursday night. They squeezed me in. As of right now, I have four appointments this week with members, and a presentation to give in Breckenridge to a small business group.*
>
> *Because I filled out that Differentiating Point survey, I realized that they were a perfect audience."*
>
> A salesperson that participated in the pilot efficiency classes

Step into Your Role

If you don't sell, it's not the product that's wrong, it's you.
Estee Lauder

Now that you have gone through an extensive process of exploration, I am going to share another insight with you. I am going to give you permission to "step into the role you were intended to play."

To quote Jim Rohn, business philosopher, speaker and author; "The most important question to ask is not, 'What am I getting?' The most important question to ask is, 'WHAT AM I BECOMING?'" I love this quote, as it causes me to reflect upon the quality and integrity of my character as it pertains to creating abundance in all facets of my life.

A concept I teach my clients is, "Step into the Role." We all have many goals for ourselves, both personally and professionally. What are you consciously doing to manifest your dreams, goals and desires... and what roles must you take on to achieve them? For example, do you have the goal to "become" a top producing sales professional? If so, then "stepping into your role" means you will be modeling the thoughts, behaviors and habits of top sales professionals in order to achieve success-in-life. By stepping into that role, you embrace it as your own... as if it were already attained... and you begin to manifest similar results.

Identify a goal you have in your life, personally or professionally. What is the role that you will "step into" in order to achieve this goal? What does the role look like, feel like, and sound like? What old behaviors will you let go of and what new behaviors will you embrace?

Disney uses a similar technique. Employees that interact with customers are called "cast members." They have fantastic costumes (not uniforms!). They are encouraged to "play the role" as if they were a cast member in a play. You too must "play the role." Be dedicated to really "feeling it" and making it your own. Take the time to note the difference in your energy and confidence levels... and enjoy the positive new results that will inevitably arrive!

> *"I have developed a niche. I attend public meetings and events that improve my visibility while meeting influential people in the neighborhood."*
>
> Survey Respondent

Always remember… you do not need to MAKE more money
"Ok Darice…so what is THIS statement all about? Obviously, I picked up this book because you promised you could HELP me to SELL MORE. And selling is about MAKING more money, right?"

Wrong.

The fact is, you do not need to "make" more money. You need to **attract more money.** The money you want, and anything else you desire, already exists. Everything ALREADY EXISTS! You do not have to "make" anything… You simply need to attract it. Remember…

- **Success is not a result of making money.**
- **Making money is the result of success.**
- **Success arrives as a result of delivering value.**
- **Value is best delivered through the channel of expressing your Differentiating Point.**

In other words, money is simply a measurement of the DEGREE OF VALUE you have provided in your market place.

"The more value I bring to the table, the more money I am going to make. The less value I bring to the table, the less money I am going to make."

Implementation

Wasn't that interesting to read? We need to move you from having been interested to taking action. Make the commitment to improve your business.

My Commitment to My Business:

- I will TAKE ACTION to make a difference in my business, TODAY!
- I stay CORE (Centered on Results Every Day).
- I EXECUTE what I am learning. I am not a perpetual student.

My greatest "AHA!" moments from this chapter were:

____

____

____

____

My 24 Hour Commitment is (what idea related to this chapter can I implement in 24 hours):

____

____

____

____

My Seven Day Commitment is:

____

____

____

____

My new standard of professional excellence or habitual way of working is:

____

____

____

____

* * * * * *

What does success look like?
It's important to note that if you are doing **the majority** of the things suggested in this chapter **the majority** of the time, THAT IS SUCCESS. It's not possible to do all things, all of the time. But if you can honestly look at yourself and say that you are doing what you need to be doing about 51% of the time, that is success.

What is in the next chapter?
Do you feel like you have an understanding of Positioning Yourself Uniquely? Have you discovered your Differentiating Point and begun implementing it in your sales efforts? The next secret of highly efficient sales professionals is revealed in Chapter 12, "Networking and The Power Triangle" Many of my clients have found that implementing some of the ideas from you just read *before* working on developing their Power Triangles made execution of The Power Triangle easier, so take some time to consider that before you read on.

12. Advanced Networking and The Power Triangle

Start "NetWeaving" Your Business Together

All things being equal, people want to do business with their friends. To climb the ladder of success, you do not need more techniques and strategies… you need more friends.
Jeffrey Gitomer, Author

How Does the "Power Triangle" Fit Into the System?

There are four Cornerstones of success. You do not necessarily need to master each of them to move on to the more advanced concepts. However, before moving on, you should be able to answer at least "neutral" instead of "disagree" on most of the Cornerstone questions on the survey in the beginning of the book. Ideally, you should "agree" to most questions. After the Cornerstones, you must get your Follow-Up systems in place.

When that is complete, you can consider the Advanced Marketing techniques. You will draw on the skills from each of the four Cornerstones and Follow-Up to their fullest potential to implement the Advanced Marketing systems.

This chapter will explore several essential topics:

M. What are Power Triangles?
N. Financial Impact
O. How to set up a Power Partnership
P. The Power Triangle
Q. Implementation

When you finish implementing the ideas within "Networking and The Power Triangle", progress to "Action Plan" which will lead you into rapid implementation and results.

What are Power Triangles?

Are you looking for new connections? New ideas? New marketing opportunities? Then it is time to "power up your business" by implementing two distinct and very effective networking methods. The first method is **The Power Partnership**. It is the most sacred of all business relationships. The second concept is the greatest networking tool of all… **The Power Triangle**.

Once I help you fully understand how these processes work independently, we will explore how they are interrelated and how one can create a greater impact for the other. We will conclude this chapter with suggestions on how to execute these two concepts simultaneously to create truly dynamic networking strategies for your business. Once you launch both of these initiatives through your businesses sales and networking efforts, I can guarantee you will be producing powerful new results.

Recall from our earlier chapter, that your database is your CASH REGISTER. Understanding its value, and spending some serious time excavating that value to bring it to the table, will be an important process to accomplish to begin executing your Power Triangles. I will show you a systematic process to accomplish this.

Financial Impact

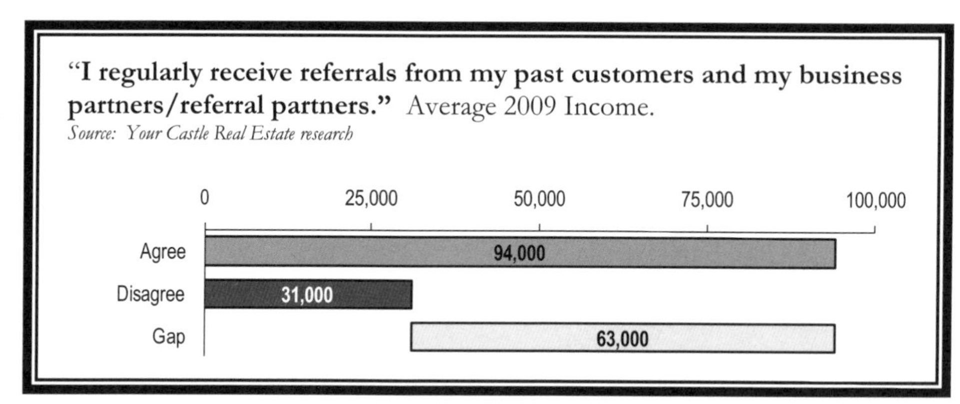

Before we examine how to set up a Power Partnership, let's take a look at the survey results to gain insight from the highest producers.

To get more insight we asked survey respondents, "What is working well for you with your business networks?"

- "What I have had to learn to do in this environment is [educate] my customers on [reasonable expectations]. This takes pressure off my team members."
- "Try to reward success rather than 'beat up' mistakes seems to work with some but not all [partners]!"

Where are the improvement opportunities with business networks?

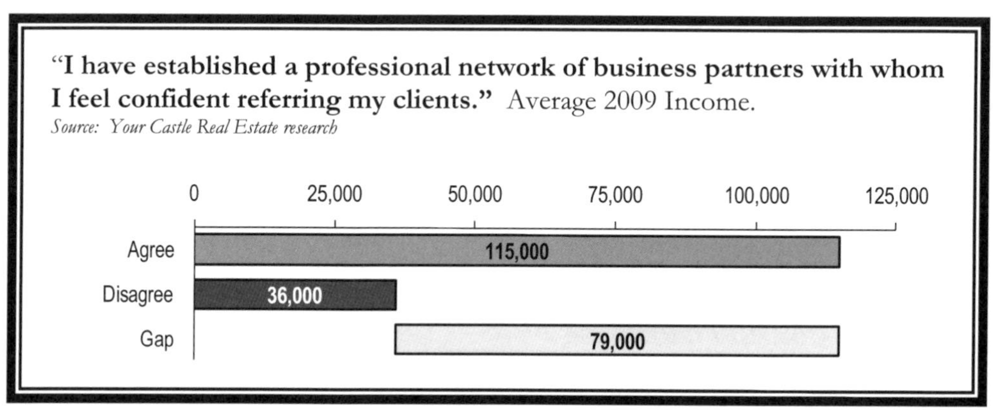

- "Referring business partners has been a big issue. Finding good service providers that will stand behind their work and their word is a tough find." (Income over $100K)
- "I do not feel like my team is established. I am having a hard time trusting them to get things done in a manner I think is sufficient."
- "Keeping them motivated, attention to detail; personally letting go/trusting."
- "We do not advertise in a traditional sense, so we have to rely on word-of-mouth and networking. This leads to many qualified buyers, locked out of financing simply because they do not know about my team."

- "I am still new to Real Estate, but am looking for honest people who want to give SERVICE... the old-fashioned way. Finding someone to TRUST with your business is a challenge when you are still learning."

How to Set Up a Power Partnership

Make the commitment NOW:

To execute your Power Triangles, you are going to need to be very clear about three commitments:

1. You will need to make a heartfelt commitment to deepen the business and personal relationships that you already have by truly getting to **know** the people currently within your network, and anyone new you may be bringing into it.
2. You will need to have a sincere dedication to understanding and living the Law of Reciprocity: "Bring something to others FIRST, knowing it will come full circle back to you."
3. You will need the genuine passion and drive to connect, connect, connect! You will need to connect into people… and you will need to connect people with other people.

If you can make these three commitments, then GET EXCITED! You are well on your way to experiencing a significant shift in your business acquisition and client retention that you have never experienced before. This chapter includes some of the most powerful information you have read yet.

> *"The "Power of Business Partnering" workshop got my creative juices flowing and I am currently implementing two key activities in my business as a result. First, a mortgage broker and I have joined forces to position and communicate the opportunity of the First time buyer's tax credit to that market. This is a market that I have tried to penetrate for a year with little success. Secondly, I have begun to look at transaction coordination services to maximize productivity."*
>
> A salesperson that participated in the pilot efficiency classes

The Power Partnership

I would venture to say that you already have a Power Partner or two… but you may not be leveraging them to their fullest capacity. Let's examine this idea of The Power Partner and explore some ways to implement it to support the growth and success of your business.

A Power Partner can be defined as, "an individual who is capable of directing business to you, either directly or indirectly, through their connections, clients or vendors." Of course, this must be reciprocal. Your Power Partner must be able to say the same of you. You then move forward together through shared marketing efforts or creative networking strategies which will be mutually beneficial to both your business and to your Power Partner's business.

Power Partners are a very effective way to boost clientele, visibility, and profitability. Why? Because in order to achieve a truly successful Power Partnership, you and your Power Partner will need to know each other's business model fairly well – at least enough to launch unique and creative endeavors that will bring you both profitable results. You create a true ally when you establish a Power Partner – someone who is as invested in the success of your business as much as you are.

Where Do You Find a Power Partner?

Your Power Partners may be friends, sales professionals, CEO's or entrepreneurs who, like yourself, are motivated to grow their business. They may be in your industry, but are more than likely in an industry inter-related to your own. You may find these potential partners in leads groups, social events, or networking meetings. You may discover them lying dormant right inside of your own database. **They may even be current clients, and that is when this process becomes incredibly valuable**.

Ultimately, many people you meet are potential Power Partners. In fact, as a business coach, I have ALWAYS been able to help my clients delve into their sphere of influence and find new ways to leverage existing relationships and establish Power Partnerships.

Admittedly, it can occasionally take some out-of-the-box thinking to establish a Power Partnership… but I guarantee you the process of exploration can be fun and ultimately financially rewarding for all involved.

Identifying & Qualifying Your Power Partners

Before approaching someone about becoming your Power Partner, do some research; even if you already know them well. The internet is a great research tool. Biographies, blogs, web pages and news articles can all give you insight into your potential Power Partners' business, personality and reputation. After you do some research, you will then want to ask yourself the following questions:

1. "Based on what this person does for a living, how can our businesses compliment each other?"
2. "Do I believe they will be willing to partner with me to launch some mutually beneficial initiatives? Will they work hard along side of me, or expect me to do all the work?"
3. "Am I comfortable with their level of integrity? Would I want to associate my name to theirs?"

Once you identify a potential Power Partner, schedule an appointment to meet with them in person specifically to discuss your intentions of the meeting. "I'm interested in exploring how you and I can create a mutually beneficial relationship between our two businesses. I feel like there may be some untapped potential there for us to look at…"

During your initial meeting, uncover your colleagues' answers to the following questions:

- How do you acquire new business?
- In what industries do you work?
- How would I direct business to you?
- What is typically a good lead for you? A good client? A great client?
- How do you qualify your prospective clients?

Once you have asked these initial questions, you will have probably identified if there is a potential fit for a Power Partnership. If so, then continue in the discovery process and ask your colleague this next series of questions:

- How can we refer business to one another?
- How can we assist the other in establishing greater visibility?
- What business initiatives can we launch together?
- What marketing efforts can we deploy together?
- What events do we each have coming up where we could promote the other's business?

Once you have established this person to be a good fit for a Power Partnership, the next step is to begin brainstorming on small initiatives to launch. As you discuss potential projects, you will begin to gain a sense of how synergistically the two of you will work together. You will have begun to establish trust and rapport.

Can you begin to see how powerful this concept can be if your selected Power Partner is a client, or a current prospect?

N introduce you to the famous and ever powerful…

The Power Triangle

The best way to get what you want is to help others get what they want
Zig Ziglar

The Law of Reciprocity states, "What you give or send out comes back to you *in kind, or in like kind*." Traditional business practices teach that the most natural (and obvious) method to attract clients would be to market to your potential audience, and conduct typical sales activities to "get to the core.". However, incorporating the power of The Law of Reciprocity brings an entirely different angle to your sales efforts. In addition to delivering valuable products and services, you also need to deliver a value to your client that reaches well beyond your usual services. That value is a heightened networking strategy I call The Power Triangle. This strategy brings unique and powerful opportunities to the table for all involved.

To launch a Power Triangle, you will need three key components.

- You – in your best, most professional form – are the first component.
- The second is your Power Partner, or another person in your database whose services you are excited to introduce to another person.
- The third component is the third person you want to connect into this powerful triad. For heightened sales, they will either be a client or a prospect.

To help you further grasp this concept, let's review the diagram below:

I could not offer my philosophy of The Power Triangle without honoring the work of Bob Littell, "Chief NetWeaver" and owner of Littell Consulting Services. Bob states there are two key concepts to Netweaving:

1. We must learn to become the strategic connector of other people and put them together in win-win relationships.
2. We must make ourselves a valuable resource.

Traditionally, sales professionals have (at least) a little ego. It's *needed* to combat the potential rejection we face every day. "It is all about me" is a common saying among some sales professionals… usually said in jest…with just a hint of sarcastic truth behind it. The concept of The Power Triangle reminds us, "It doesn't need to be about me." In fact, the most successful sales professionals incorporate The Power Triangle naturally and without thinking twice about it.

They know that real success comes from a willingness to serve. Through service we earn respect, allegiance and an abundance of business.

Deployed correctly, The Power Triangle cultivates relationships to the point of deepened allegiance, a heightened number of referrals, reciprocal business, valuable masterminded concepts and much more.

Excavating Your Sphere of Influence

It is time to put this into practice. As you excavate your database, examine each contact. Ask yourself:

- Is there someone I know who could benefit from this person?
- Is there someone I know who this person can benefit from?
- Would I personally do business with this person? (If not, do not refer…)
- Can I trust them to care for my clients or potential clients?

You may already be considering who your potential Power Partners are. You may be mentally scanning your sphere of influence and making a list of acquaintances, service providers, clients and friends who can direct business your way, and to whom you can direct business as well.

To help you with the upcoming exercise, let's say that you sell accounting services to small business. In seeking to identify your Power Partners, you take your leads group into consideration. You discover that there are five key people within your leads group who you feel hold great potential for this endeavor. Let's say that at this point, none of these individuals are clients of yours, yet. Here is your list:

<u>My potential Power Partners:</u>

- Mark, Insurance Broker
- Mitch, Financial Planner
- Beth, Estate Planning Attorney
- John, Realtor
- David, Mortgage Broker

Next, in order to begin creating your Power Triangles, you will now make a list of your top clients… as well as your top prospects:

<u>My "A" Clients and "A & B" Prospects</u>

- George, owner of a spa and hair salon
- Lisa, owner of a catering company
- Denise, owner of a dog grooming shop
- Laura, owner of a bridal shop
- Gloria, owner of a housekeeping services business
- Stacey, owner of a consulting company offering personal/in-home tech support

To deploy The Power Triangle, consider how to connect each of these eleven individuals together. Begin making those connections over coffee, cocktails, client appreciation events, etc. **Again, the end goal is for you to create a deeper connection "with" and "to" all eleven contacts by connecting them together. You are potentially provide them with value that reaches well beyond their use of the products and services your accounting company provides.**

Let's examine the needs of only six of these eleven individuals and thoughtfully consider who could benefit from meeting whom:

Mark, Insurance Broker	**Beth, Estate Planning Attorney**	**Laura, Bridal Shop Owner**
Ask yourself, "Who can Mark most benefit from connecting with?" *Mitch, Financial Planner Beth, Estate Planning Attorney *John, Realtor David, Mortgage Broker	Ask yourself, "Who can Beth most benefit from connecting with?" *John, Realtor David, Mortgage Broker *Laura, Bridal Shop Owner	Ask yourself, "Who can Laura most benefit from connecting with?" George, Hairdresser Lisa, Caterer Mark, Insurance Broker Mitch, Financial Planner *Beth, Estate Planning Attorney John, Realtor David, Mortgage Broker
John, Realtor	**Stacey, Personal Tech Support**	**Mitch, Financial Planner**
Ask yourself, "Who can John most benefit from connecting with?" David, Mortgage Broker George, Hairdresser Lisa, Caterer Denise, Dog Grooming Shop Laura, Bridal Shop Owner Gloria, Housekeeping Business *Stacey, Personal Tech Support *Mark, Insurance Broker *Mitch, Financial Planner *Beth, Estate Planning Attorney	Ask yourself, "Who can Stacey most benefit from connecting with?" Mark, Insurance Broker Mitch, Financial Planner Beth, Estate Planning Attorney *John, Realtor David, Mortgage Broker George, Hairdresser Lisa, Caterer Denise, Dog Grooming Shop Laura, Bridal Shop Owner Gloria, Housekeeping Business	Ask yourself, "Who can Mitch most benefit from connecting with? Beth, Estate Planning Attorney *John, Realtor David, Mortgage Broker George, Hairdresser Lisa, Caterer Denise, Dog Grooming Shop Laura, Bridal Shop Owner Gloria, Housekeeping Business Stacey, Personal Tech Support *Mark, Insurance Broker

Based on the table above, incorporating only eleven people in your sphere, you have identified a wealth of Power Triangles that could be created… and YOU will be the force behind orchestrating these connections.

Your next step is to physically connect these people with each other so they can network and determine how they can synergistically work together to get business done. Then… once your Power Triangle is launched, you simply stay connected to these individuals as you always have, allowing them the space and time to determine their professional destiny together. YOUR job is to be the CONNECTOR – their job is to run with it. Of course, as you get connected to more and more people, you will begin seeking to create an even greater number of opportunities to help others grow their business….all the while knowing that you are deepening their allegiance to you and YOUR BUSINESS, as well.

- ✓ Do you think that your clients will appreciate your thoughtfulness to help them grow their business and create a deeper allegiance with you?
- ✓ Do you think your A& B Prospects will convert from prospect to client after you have given them an opportunity to grow their business?
- ✓ Do you think your leads group participants will consider becoming clients themselves as well as referring others to you more proactively if you put them in front of people on this capacity?

Now…can you see how powerful this process can really be?

Let's take a moment to explore your own network and see what Power Partners and Power Triangle you can create.

A. List 5 clients who are in sales or are in their own business, who you can promote:

____

____

____

____

____

Who can benefit from meeting them? Who can they benefit by meeting?

____

____

____

____

____

B. List 5 prospects who are in sales or own their own business who you would like to promote:

____

____

____

____

____

Who con benefit from meeting them? Who can they benefit by meeting?

____

____

____

____

____

At first blush, The Law of Reciprocity and The Power Triangle may appear to go against the traditional way of doing business. But as you can see, this concept…when deployed alongside traditional sales and marketing efforts, can be so powerful that you may never turn back to doing business without it. That is because ultimately, **business is about relationships. People want to do business with people with whom they have relationships. People they know, like, and trust.**

In conclusion, by establishing Power Triangles you are:

- Positioned as the connector of great people for great reasons.
- Bringing heightened value to your clients, prospects and Power Partners by helping them generate more business for themselves.
- Expanding your sphere of influence, as one connection begets another.
- Creating an allegiance between your sphere and yourself that runs so deeply they would never even consider doing business with anyone but you.

Now, go dig into your sphere of influence and start analyzing the potential laying dormant inside. I can promise you, the results will be electrifying!

******

Implementation

Wasn't that interesting to read? We need to move you from having been interested to taking action. Make the commitment to improve your business.

My Commitment to My Business

- I will TAKE ACTION to make a difference in my business, TODAY!
- I stay C.O.R.E. (Centered on Results Every Day).
- I EXECUTE what I am learning. I am not a perpetual student.

My greatest "AHA!" moments from this chapter were:

____

My 24 hour Commitment is (what idea related to this chapter can I implement in 24 hours):

My Seven Day Commitment is:

My new standard of professional excellence or habitual way of working is:

* * * * * *

What does success look like?
It's important to note that if you are doing **the majority** of the things suggested in this chapter **the majority** of the time, THAT IS SUCCESS. It's not possible to do all things, all of the time. But if you can honestly look at yourself and say that you are doing what you need to be doing about 51% of the time, that is success.

What is in the next chapter?

The eighth secret of highly efficient sales professionals is revealed in Chapter 13, "The 90-Day Action Plan" The next chapter is all about execution: planning, prioritizing and implementing your top priorities in 90-day increments Get excited! You are about to establish a laser focus and clarity that will move your sales business to the next level.

13.Launching Your 90-Day Action Plan

Tactical Planning and Execution of Your Top Priorities

The only real competition you have is the competition between your disciplined and undisciplined mind.
- James Author Ray

Putting it All Together

We have covered a great deal of ground in this book. You have identified a few key things you want to implement and have probably even taken some significant steps toward incorporating many of these systems and ideas into your sales business. Using the implementation pages at the end of each chapter,

Remember, if you have achieved a 51% shift in executing even one of these suggestions, you have experienced success! Many low producing sales people seem to have lots of time to talk about how "broken" their business is. Interestingly, it is these same individuals who also complain about being "too busy" to fix it. Undoubtedly, they are focusing their time and energy on non-dollar producing activities and simultaneously lacking a real focus on what the top priorities.

What if they shifted their energy expenditure? What if they took proactive action over the next 90 days to implement the systems that would support them in measurable growth? What if they made the necessary changes NOW to take their business to the next level? How different would their business look in 90 days?

> *"In the past I have spent a substantial amount of time on a yearly business plan and on daily tasks but did not correlate the two. After your classes, I now see a bridge between daily, weekly and quarterly activities that lead to the accomplishment of longer-term goals. The big goals do not seem insurmountable when they are broken down into smaller tasks."*
>
> A sales person who participated in the pilot efficiency classes.

How different will YOUR business look in 90 days?

Congratulations on slowing down enough to pour over the pages of this book. You took the time and found the energy to consider what changes would be purposeful and meaningful for your business. Now… it is time to put everything together into one simple 90-day action plan.

Why does Efficiency by Design use 90-Day Action Planning?

I use action planning as opposed to business planning because I feel sales professionals need a simplified, executable plan to keep them on track over short periods of time.

In my experience, I have found that elaborate business plans may be too much for the sales-hearted as you flutter about your day from one appointment to the next. After all, your main objectives will always be to create visibility, engage in appointments and close deals. However, as you have discovered in this book, there are critical systems that you need in your business to support you in executing your most important activities. If I show you how to establish a simple, laser focused action plan to support you in working your systems while simultaneously selling, you will be much more likely to execute the activities required to boost your sales. You will also be less likely to experience the "sales roller coaster ride" by ensuring you have a continuous stream of prospects and therefore a continuous stream of business.

Yes, it's critical for you to know what you want your financial security to look like in 5-10 years. But that is not what I am here to do. My objective is to:

1. Help you identify your income goal and your required quota for a twelve month window which we will use as a measuring stick.
2. Keep you on track from one quarter to the next with a clear picture of the tactical steps required to *attain* your annual financial and productivity goals.

By supporting you to create systems, add structure, and establish new habits NOW, I can help you attain the income level you desire.

There are three elements to your 90 Day Action Plan. Take a moment to review those elements in detail, and jot down some initial items that cross your mind that you would like to work on.

1. Goals:

1. Financial:
   How much money do you want to NET in the next 12 months?

   ____

2. Productivity:
   What is your *required* quota, as dictated by your company?

   ____

   What is your *desired* quota, as dictated by your financial goals? Regardless of what you sell, figure out how much you need to sell and at what price point you need to sell it on a quarterly basis in order to reach your desired annual financial goal.

   ____

2. Action Plan

What do you feel needs strengthening with these four key areas of your business?

1. Client Acquisition
   Activities might include:
   - Targeting new prospects
   - Prospecting activities
   - Getting better at setting appointments
   - Improving conversion efficiency
   - Acquiring referrals
   - Power Partners and Power Triangles
   - Associated projects

What things would you like to focus on?

____

____

____

2. Client Relationships
   Focus areas might include:
   - Reconnecting with orphaned clients
   - Increasing revenue per client
   - Power Partners and Power Triangles
   - Associated projects

   What things would you like to focus on?

____

____

____

3. Marketing & Visibility
   Focus areas might include:
   - Executing Sales Tracks
   - Executing Marketing Campaigns
   - Add future list from business plan

   What things would you like to focus on?

____

____

____

4. Administrative Functions and Systems
   Focus areas might include:
   - Time management
   - Database Management
   - Email Management
   - New systems
   - Accounting processes
   - Flow charts
   - Checklists

   What things would you like to focus on?

   ____

   ____

   ____

5. Other Important Items
   Focus areas might include:
   - Personal Development
   - Professional Development and Education

   What things would you like to focus on?

   ____

   ____

   ____

3. Stay CORE (Centered on Results Every Day)

There are eleven key items I consider to be your CORE activities for your business. These are listed below. Your 90-Day Action Plan already includes these items for your regular reference. Staying CORE means you are executing the eleven actions fairly consistently, but there is always room for improvement. Select those items you know you need to give more attention to over the next 90 days:

1. Honor your time blocking, including appointments you schedule for daily prep, Happy Hour, completions, and deliverables.
2. Keep your environments orderly for highest functionality, both mentally and physically.
3. Practice strong Daily Disciplines. Use your CORE Weekly Plan to help you do this.
4. Track your progress weekly. How many closed transactions and how many new clients did you have?
5. Stay close to your database. Update with new contacts and important information as quickly as possible.
6. Incorporate "Happy Hour" daily – Schedule phone time to set appointments at least 5 hours per week
7. Get out that door. Predetermine your number of appointments, fill that book and get out that door!
8. Live Your Differentiating Point and keep Power Triangles "top of mind" in your prospecting efforts.
9. Work your Sales Tracks and launch your Marketing Campaigns
10. Plan and prioritize. Do this daily. Regularly reference and execute from your 90 Day Action Plan.
11. Keep infusing positive beliefs and intentions into your business.

What things would you like to focus on?

____

____

____

Planning... in Four Easy Steps

What you are about complete is an easy, clear and powerful action plan. Remember, my goal is to keep it super simple: to make sure you will execute, execute, execute!

In the Action Plan provided below,

1. Scan each of the suggested categories on the left and their related segments of your business.

2. Record the goals you have for each of category over the next 90 days.

3. Brainstorm and write down the tasks or actions required to reach your goals. Select no more than five.

4. Indicate a timeframe or deadline required for the attainment of each task or action.

This form can be also be used on a weekly or monthly basis as well.

The 90-Day Action Plan   For the Dates of:

ANNUAL GOALS:
Financial:
Productivity:

BUSINESS SEGMENTS	90 DAY GOALS	TASKS /ACTION ITEMS	DEADLINES
CLIENT ACQUISITION (Developing new revenue) • Identifying Target Prospects • Prospecting Activity • Appointment Setting • Conversions • Acquiring Referrals • Power Partners & Power Triangles • Follow-Up Skills • Associated Projects			
CLIENT RETENTION (Expanding current relationships) • Re-connecting with Orphaned Clients • Increasing Revenue per Client • Power Partners and Power Triangles • Associated Projects			
MARKETING & VISIBILITY • Sales Tracks • Marketing Campaigns • Advertising Initiatives • Leads Groups /Mastermind Groups • Associations & Volunteering • Event Planning • Power Partners and Power Triangles • Associated Projects			
ADMINISTRATIVE FUNCTIONS • Time Management • Database Management • Email Management • Daily Disciplines • CORE Weekly Action Plan • Accounting • Systems & Processes • Checklists • Flow Charts • Associated Projects			

Professional Development & Education Classes, Designations, Training	**Personal Development** Self-Care Needs, Personal Goals, Family Time, Personal Time

STAY CORE

1. I honor my time blocking, including appointments for Daily Prep, Happy Hour and Completions.
2. I keep my environments orderly for highest functionality, both mentally and physically.
3. I practice strong Daily Disciplines. I use my CORE Weekly Plan to help me execute my priorities.
4. I track my sales results. I know how many closed transactions and new clients I have, weekly.
5. I stay connected into my database and update it with new contacts and information immediately.
6. I incorporate "Happy Hour" daily. I call and schedule appointments at least 5 hours per week.
7. I get "out that door". I predetermine the number of appointments I need and fill my book weekly.
8. I live my Differentiating Point and I keep Power Triangles "top of mind" in my prospecting efforts.
9. I work my Sales Tracks and launch my Marketing Campaigns
10. I plan and prioritize daily and quarterly. I regularly execute from my 90 Day Action Plan.
11. I infuse positive beliefs and intentions into my business.

This form can be accessed from my website at www.EfficiencyByDesignOnline.com. Download and customize this for your unique requirements. Consider typing your plan and sending it to a printer to expand the size and laminate. You can hang it on your office wall for quick reference.

Need some help identifying tasks for your action plan?

What follows is a list of the survey questions we introduced to you throughout this book. These may give you additional clues as to some action items you may want to incorporate into your action plan:

A. Time Mastery

- I feel comfortable with the amount of time I am spending on administrative tasks.
- I spend at least 50% of my work hours on dollar productive activities and at least 25% of that time on new sales.
- I am very good about performing only dollar productive activities during my most dollar productive hours.
- I have adequate time for relaxation, family time, personal time, and time to pursue my personal interests.
- I am able to avoid needless interruptions during my workday and stay focused on what matters most in my business.

What things would you like to focus on?

___

___

B. Piles to Files

- I have a system in place to track progress on current transactions as well as potential business.
- I have an effective filing system that allows me to keep clutter from my workspace. I easily find documents I need in seconds.
- I have a system in place to manage my email. I only tend to important and urgent email during dollar productive hours.

What things would you like to focus on?

___

___

___

C. Daily Disciplines

- I have tools and systems in place to help me stay on track with my daily, weekly and monthly priorities.
- I pre-plan my day and my week before it begins.
- I conduct my daily business using a schedule that works well for me.

What things would you like to focus on?

___

___

___

D. Falling in Love with Your Database

- I maintain one database where I enter all of my contacts
- I have a very clear way to qualify my prospects.
- I maintain client records so I can capture customer preferences important dates, and record key information from conversations.
- I update my database at least once a week with new names I have acquired to prevent "business card pile-up" and loss of follow-up.

What things would you like to focus on?

___

___

___

At this point, pause for a moment. If you did not score at least a "B" on the four Cornerstones, finish your plan with what you currently have and work on implementation for the next ninety days. Then retake the survey and see how you have improved.

When you score at least a "B" on the Cornerstones, then move on to "Follow-Up."

E. Mastering the Art of Follow-Up

- I set the appropriate number of appointments every week to reach my sales goals.
- I know the number of new people I need to add to my database and marketing campaign every month, and add them.
- I qualify potential customers using a needs-analysis approach. I do not waste energy on the wrong clients.
- My past clients receive consistent communication from me on a regularly basis via social media, mail, email and phone.
- I have a high-touch campaign to follow-up with people I have just met, or clients that have demonstrated an immediate need.
- I have a passive marketing campaign that I use to stay connected to past clients, as well as prospects that are not ready to buy just yet.

What things would you like to focus on?

___

___

___

At this point, please pause for a moment. If you did not score at least a "B" on Follow-Up, finish your plan with what you currently have and work on implementation for the next ninety days. Then retake the survey and see how you have improved.

If you have at least a "B" on the Cornerstones and Follow-Up, then move on to the Advanced Marketing techniques, "Positioning Yourself Uniquely" and "Networking and The Power Triangle."

F. Marketing and Differentiating Yourself

- I am pleased with the designations I currently hold or industry-specific training I have completed.
- I stay up to date on market trends and understand how they affect my business.
- I make sure my education includes sales training and professional training, as well as industry related and required training, to continuously improve myself professionally.
- I have discovered how I can differentiate myself in this industry and my marketing efforts and products reflect that.

What things would you like to focus on?

____

____

____

G. Networking and The Power Triangle

- I have established a polished and professional network of business partners. I feel confident referring my clients to them.
- I regularly receive referrals from my business partners, referral partners and past clients.
- I personally ensure that my clients receive responses to all inquiries, whether I am personally handling the inquiry or not.

What things would you like to focus on?

____

____

____

H. The Ninety Day Action Plan

- I know the key things I must do daily, weekly and monthly to move my business forward. I do these key things consistently.
- I have a clear vision and direction for my business that I am passionate about achieving.
- I stay aware of trends occurring in my marketplace. My business plan is flexible. I can incorporate these changes into my business rather than feeling victimized by them.
- I set annual goals for myself in writing and check progress on them at least monthly.

What things would you like to focus on?

____

____

____

* * * * * *

Use this table as a quick summary of what your points of focus will be over the next few days. The quick summary:

Week	Focus area
1	
2	
3	
4	
5	
6	
7	
8	
9	
10	
11	
12	

That is it! It really was not that hard, was it?

Find an accountability partner with whom you can share your plan. Sit down for a few minutes each week to track your progress. Block out time in three months to re-take the assessment and see how far you have progressed.

UNLOCKED workshops and seminars are available throughout the year. These seminars help you execute everything you read in this book into your business, with the added benefit of interaction with your peers and a business coach.

For information, or to reserve your seat at our next seminar, please call 303-862-7416 or visit us online at www.EfficiencyByDesignOnline.com.

14. Appendix A – Using Outlook Effectively

By Drew Shope
Founding Partner,
Thrive Social Media, LLC
www.ThiveSocialMedia.com

A crucial part of your business is maintaining a current, well-planned database. Many sales professionals overlook this critical success driver. In our prior book, *Thrive: How Realtors Can Succeed in a Down Market*, we were able to measure the financial impact of utilizing a database. Sales professionals with a contact management system made $52,000 more per year then those who did not ($137,000 versus $85,000). Will the simple addition of a database increase your income this much? No, but this change, coupled with other critical success drivers, will help you increase your income dramatically.

With any database system, it will increase your sales only if you use it regularly. It works if it becomes a seamless part of your life and routine. You can use whatever system your heart desires, as long as you use it effectively. Outlook is a good choice for a contact database, but it is not the only option. We know a very high producer that is still successfully using a well organized shoebox with recipe cards after nearly thirty years in the business. As long as you are using only one organizational system and using it well, you will see the results.

Why Is the Database Essential?

In real estate industry, the average time for a prospect to go from thinking about buying or selling a house to actually going to closing is between 9 and 21 months. In addition to the challenge of the long sales cycle, 80% of sales happen on the 5th to 12th contact with the prospect.

Staying in touch with your prospects and clients is critical for your success. High production sales people have processes to support this consistent follow-up. These ratios will be different in other industries, but most relationship sales require multiple contacts over time to achieve sales success.

We chose to discuss Outlook for this book for three reasons.

1. It is easy to use.
2. Most people already have it on their computer (though most use it only for email.)
3. It is a very powerful and universally used program that can manage your contacts, your daily task list and so much more.

The screenshots and specific click-by-click steps are all in Outlook 2003. Many readers may have Outlook 2007, which has a few extra features and a slightly different look. This appendix will review several topics:

"Foundation" topics

- Email
- Tasks
- Notes
- Contact management
- Calendar and appointments

"Intermediate" topics

- Dragging emails
- Creating email folders
- Task lists
- Database views
- Master category lists
- Mail merge

Foundation Outlook Topics

Email

Most people use Outlook only to manage their email. It can be cumbersome to use one program for email, another for your calendar, and yet another for your contacts. Outlook can do all three tasks. Let's start by looking at how Outlook can help with your email:

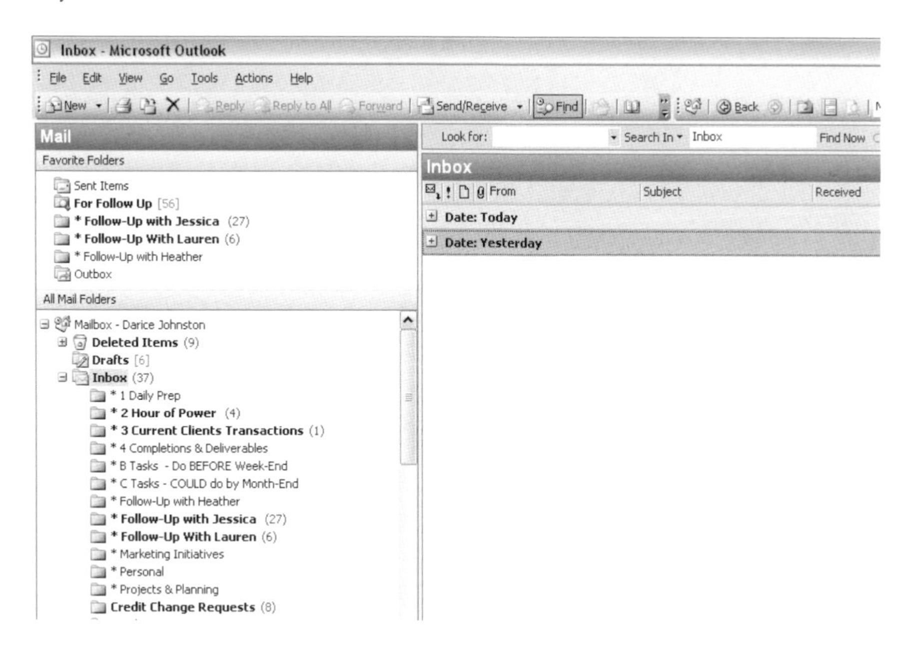

We will not go over the specifics of getting your email plugged into Outlook. If you need to complete this, go to Google and ask for a guide. It will likely be there. For example, if you have a Gmail account that you want to view in Outlook, type "Gmail outlook setup"…

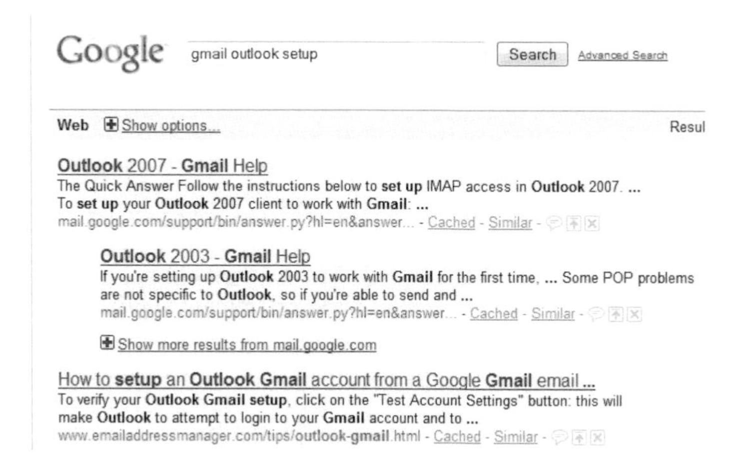

… and you will find a step by step guide.

Follow the directions, and once set up, there are some great ways to manage your emails as they arrive. Use rules to flag the email based on qualifiers that you select. For example:

- Emails with the word "Interested" automatically go into a folder named "Leads"
- Emails from clients go into an "A List" folder.
- Emails with spam keywords like "Discount Pharmacy" go to the trash.

This will make your inbox easier to manage. Applying rules is simple:

1. Click on File > New > Folder while in the Mail screen.
2. Name this folder whatever you would like (e.g., A Clients, B Clients)
3. Click on Tools, then Rules and Alerts.

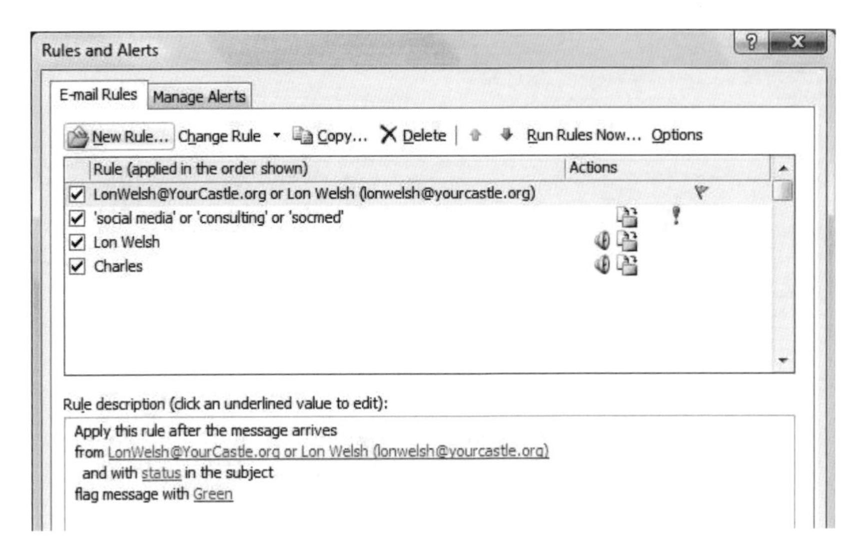

4. Click on New Rule (that is near the upper left corner). You will see a dialogue box:

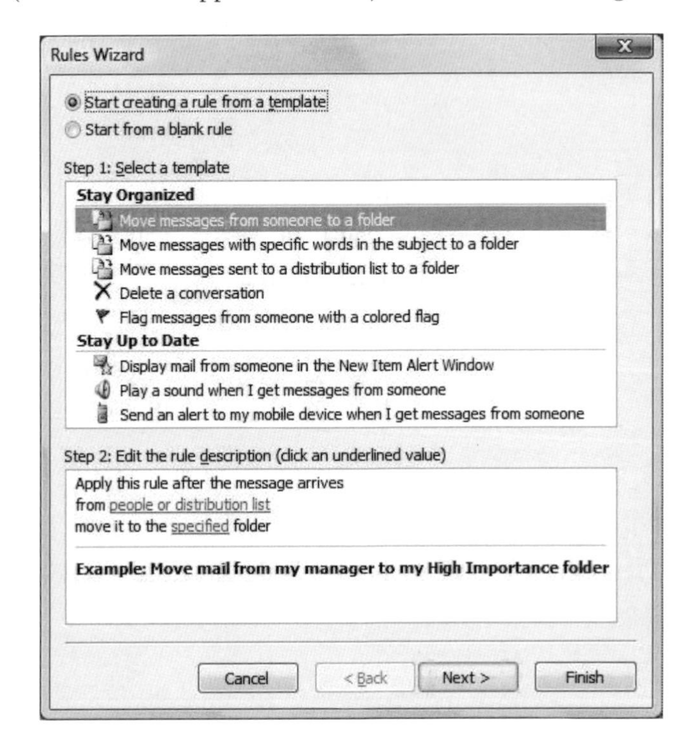

5. Click on the blue text in the bottom window.
    - If you want to have a rule associated with a particular email contact, you need to have that contact already entered into the system.
    - Another thing you could do is have anyone's email from a specific distribution list route into a certain folder.
    - This way, instead of having to add a person to a category distribution list as well as to the rule, you could *just* add them to the distribution list.

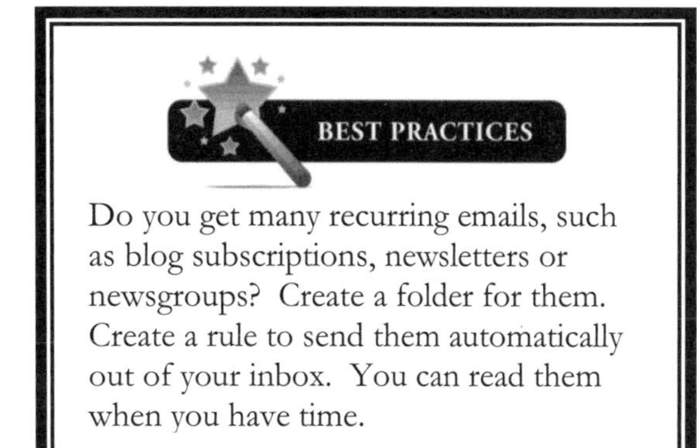

Do you get many recurring emails, such as blog subscriptions, newsletters or newsgroups? Create a folder for them. Create a rule to send them automatically out of your inbox. You can read them when you have time.

You can also create rules from a specific email.

1. Right-click on the message
2. Click on 'create rule'
3. Follow the wizard.

This is a great way to organize automated emails such as newsletter subscriptions.

Contacts

The contacts portion of Outlook is arguably the most important feature of the whole program. It is important to have all your contacts in one place. There are several ways to import ACT files, or your Gmail contacts. If you are migrating all of your contacts into one place, it is going to take some time. Be patient. The pay off will be worth it.

Entering in a new contact is simple.

1. While on the "Contacts" screen, click on the "New" button in the upper-left corner:

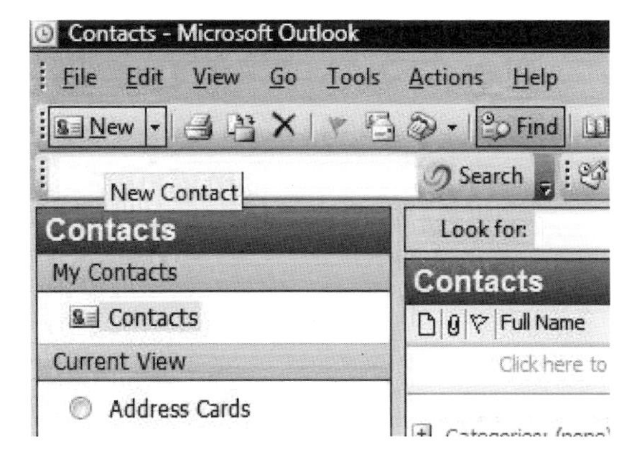

This will bring up the "enter new contact" dialogue box:

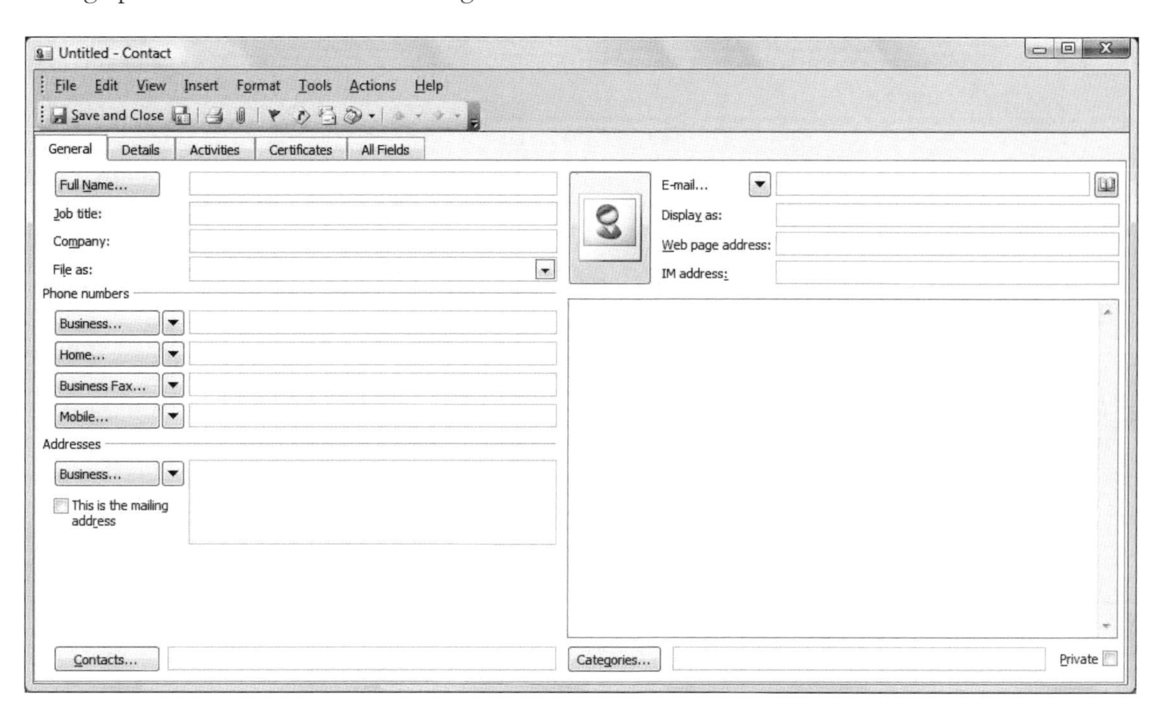

2. Enter name, phone, email and other information.
3. Be sure to pay attention to the highlighted fields below:

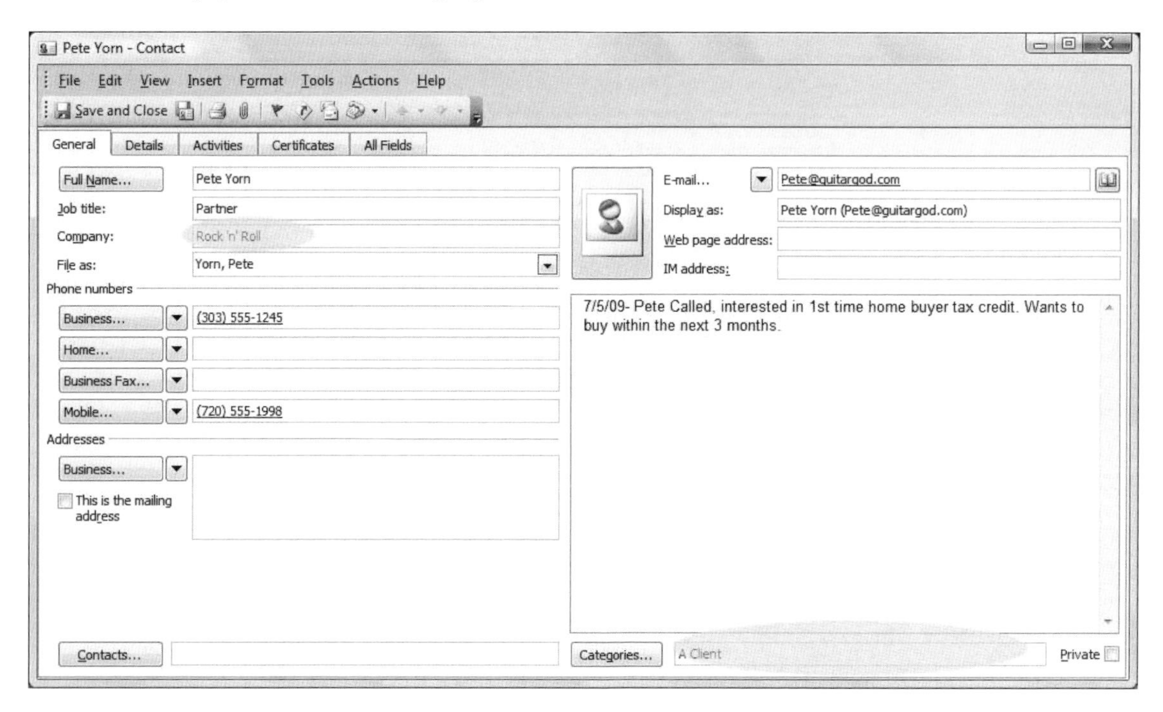

4. Company (near the upper left corner) and Categories (near the bottom right of the pop-up box) are quick ways to sort your contacts. See previous chapters for suggestions of the types of categories to use.

5. Pay attention to the notes area above the Categories field. This is a very powerful tool. While speaking with the contact, have their contact card open and take notes. This way, you can have a long, continuous conversation instead of many choppy ones; you know right where you left off.
6. If you do not have their contact card open while having the conversation, be sure to transfer this information to the contact card along with the date and time of the discussion.

> *Tip: When you are reading emails, you can drag the email onto the "Contacts" tab on the left and it will automatically drop the email into the notes field for the contact. If they are not already a contact, it will create one for that email address.*

To send an email to a specific category (such as all of your 'A Clients'), right click while in the "Contacts" screen:

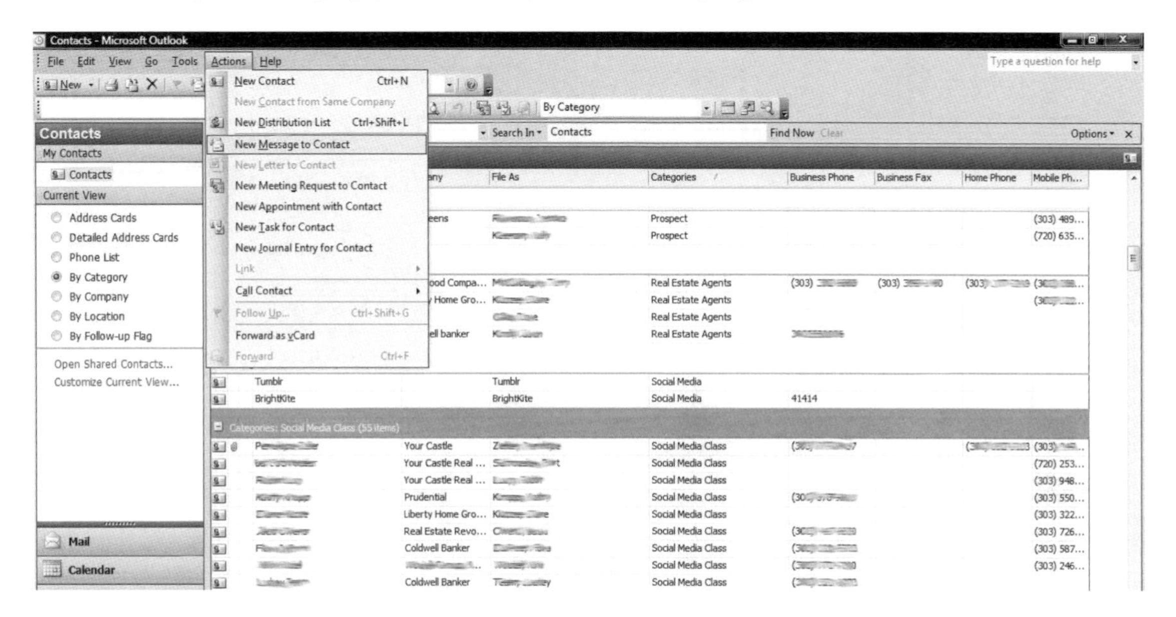

We recommend putting all the addresses into the BCC field instead of the CC field. Then it is not obvious that the recipient is a part of a large mailing. It also helps keep their information more private. Put your own address in the 'To' field. Alternatively, use the mail merge feature discussed later in this chapter.

Calendar

Time blocking, as stated earlier in this book, is a key tool for success. Here is an example of how time blocking a schedule can look:

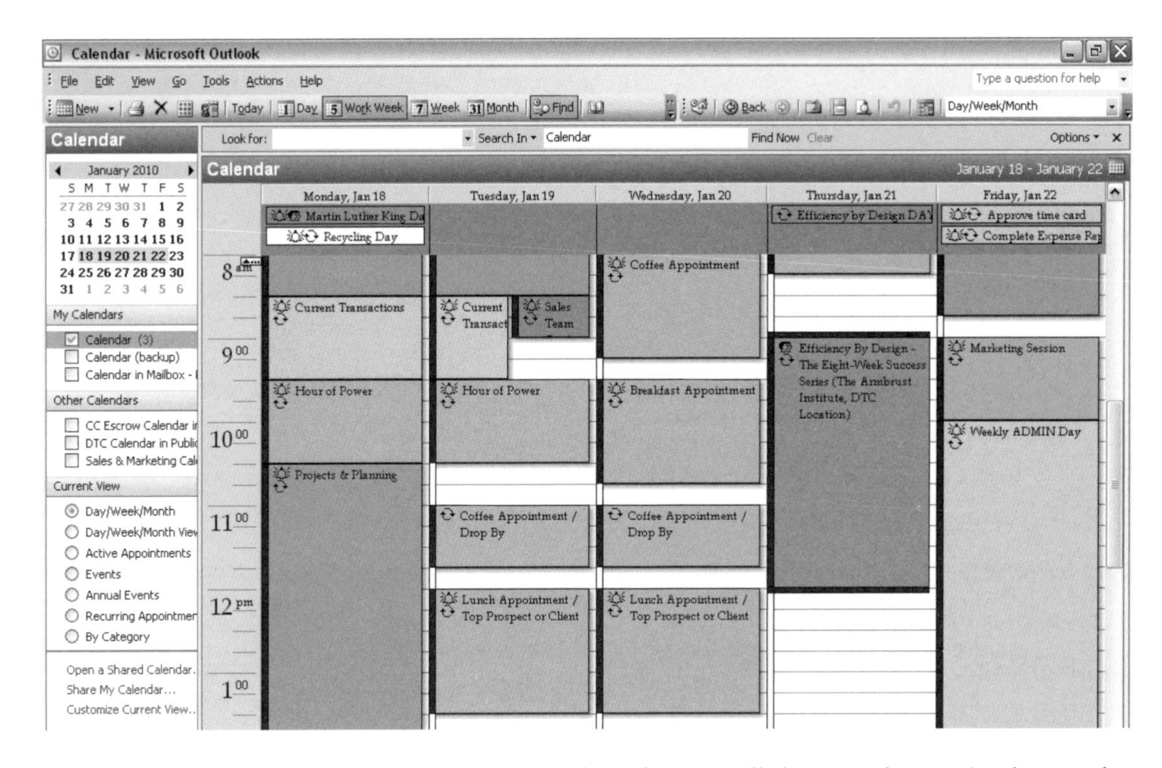

We will not go over the importance of time blocking again here, but we will show you how to implement these tactics.

Creating a new Appointment

While on the "Calendar" screen, simply click on the "New" button in the top-left corner:

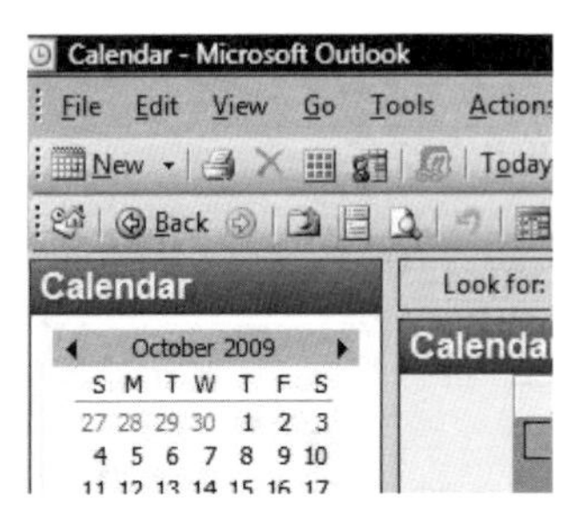

Clicking on "New" will bring up this screen for a new appointment:

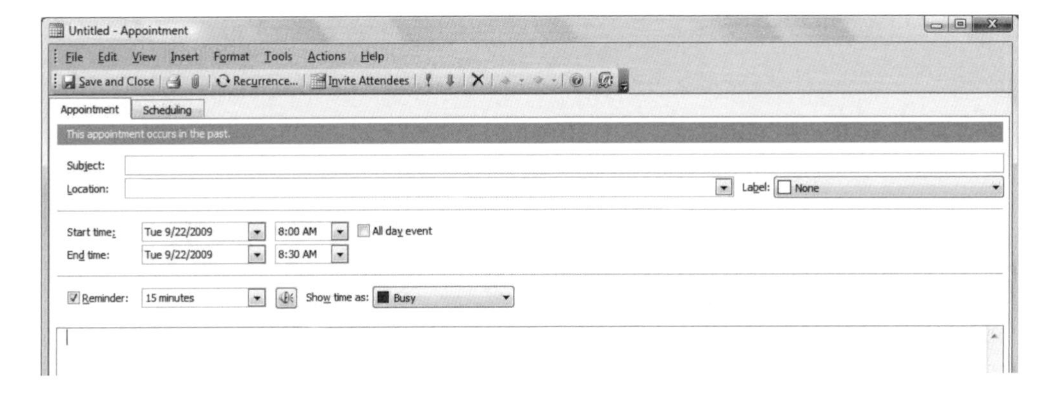

Use the "Label" dropdown on the right side to color code your activities. The colors are defaulted to random events (Purple's default tag is Birthday, for example). All you need to adjust is the color. Use the color scheme from the book (see chapter 6, Time Mastery).

A helpful tool is the "Recurrence" feature. That button is near the top of the dialogue box, just under the menu bar (see the screen print above).

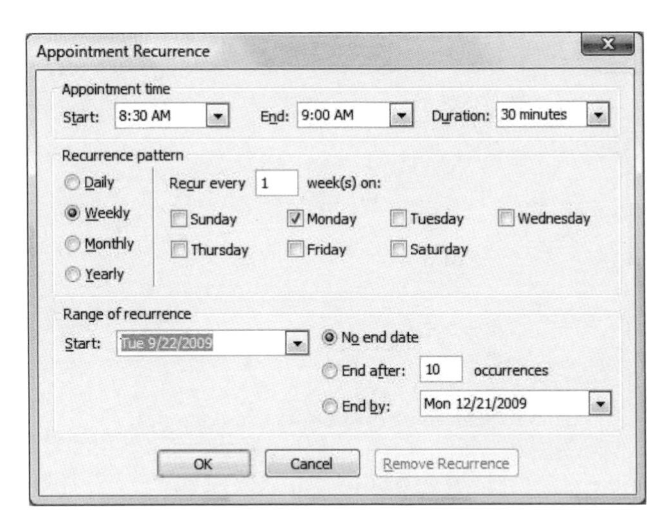

This is a simple way to make sure you do not forget to call people for their birthdays, anniversaries, etc. The "All-Day Events" event can be useful for some situations, too. The All Day Events allow you to use an alarm, and will always "float" at the top of the day's schedule. It is all about personal preference. See what works best for you.

Tasks

The task list can be your best friend or worst enemy. Again, it comes down to personal preference. Drew Shope cannot stand the task feature of Outlook, and sees it as an "annoying encumbrance." Another author has a constantly running task list that keeps him focused. Another has a maximum of three tasks that *must* be done that day. It is all about your personal taste.

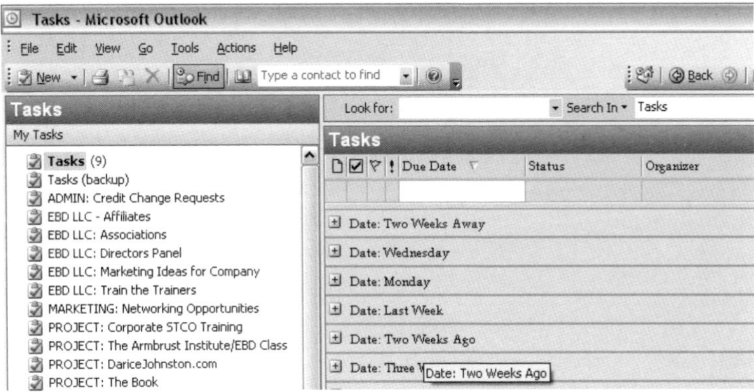

Click on the "Task" tab to get to the Task List screen.

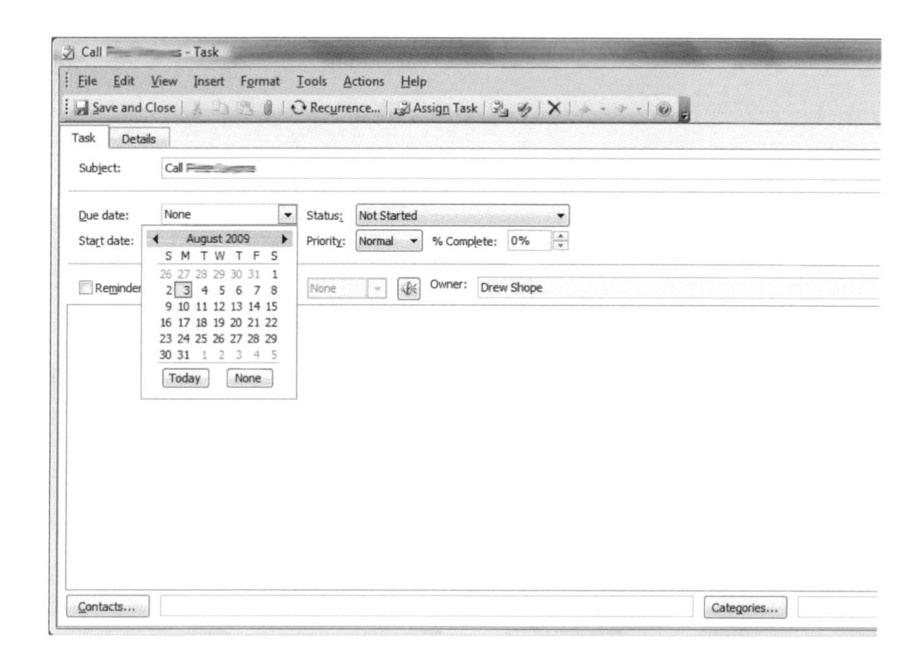

The task set up is straightforward. This also has an option to set a recurrence.

Another helpful feature of using the task list instead of the "All Day Event" is the ability to assign tasks to anyone in your database. This can be a very effective way to manage your time as well as your assistants' time. Whomever you assign the task to will receive a similar email, with the option to Accept or Decline:

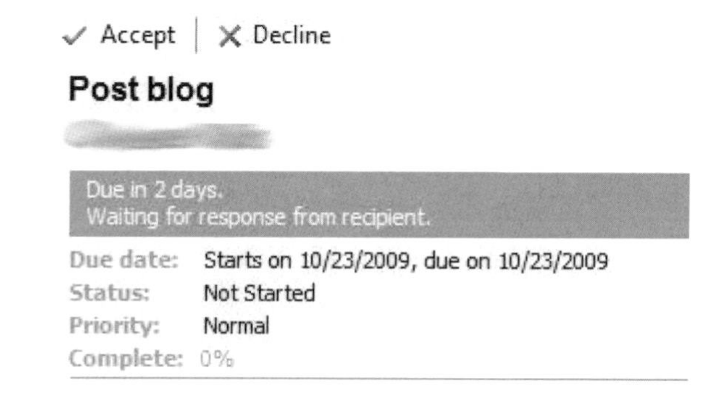

There are a number of features in the Task section that you may or may not find useful. For example, the "Assign Task" function may be very useful if want to make sure that a vendor partner completes a task that is important to closing your deal even though that tasks is not your direct responsibility. Assigning a priority or category may also be very helpful in deciding on how to manage a task.

Notes

The other feature we frequently use in Outlook is the Notes section. Often overlooked, this little feature has saved us a lot of time scrambling for a pen and paper while on a call.

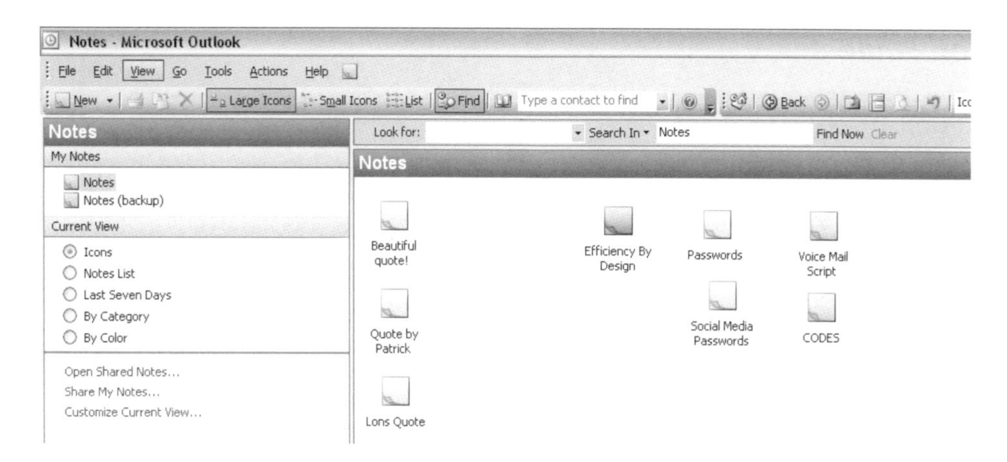

To get to the notes section, click on the little yellow square that vaguely resembles a pad of sticky notes. It is really just a quick type pad, and you can drag emails, contacts, tasks or calendar items to the notes field. Notes are handy and very simple.

Intermediate Outlook Topics

Dragging Email to Other Components

Outlook has the ability to drag an email to another tab (such as Calendar, Contacts or Tasks). Outlook will automatically enter the information from email accordingly. For example, by dragging an email from a client onto the "Contacts" tab on the left, Outlook will drop the email's contents into the "notes" area of that person's contact file. If you do not have them entered in as a contact yet, it will create a contact file with their email and name, if available. Simply click and drag the specific email from the Mail Folder window and drop it wherever you would like.

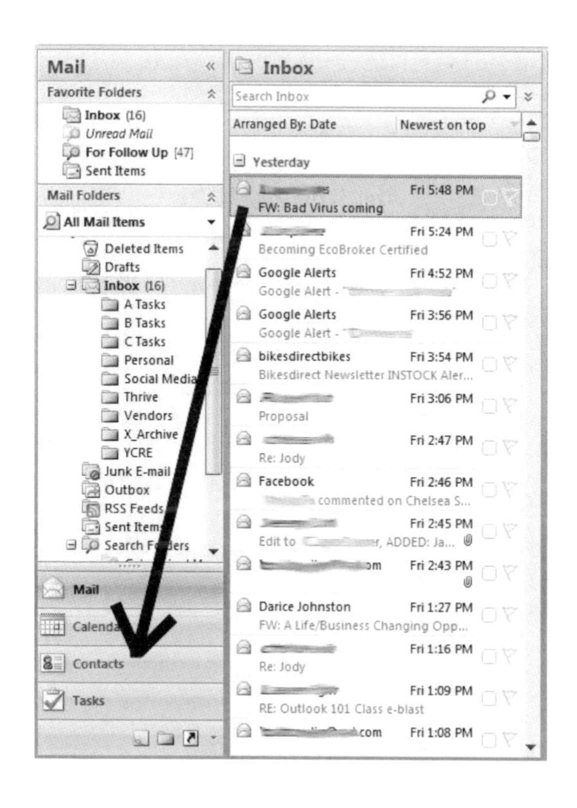

This can help you track conversations with everyone with whom you talk. Instead of spending several minutes tracking down a person's emails to figure out what they are talking about, you can get into a habit of placing them in one spot.

If you drag the email to the Calendar or Task tabs, it will create a new Event or Task, accordingly. Again, you could set an all day event or task to have that email floating on the top or bottom of your calendar screen, making it an easy reminder.

Creating Email Folders

This process is straightforward. At the top of Outlook, click on File, select New and then click on Folder. This will bring up a directory of all folders already created.

1. Type in a name for the new folder
2. Set the folder type (for this example, leave "Folder contains" as Mail and Post Items).
3. Select the folder you wish to create a subfolder under (for example, to create an "A Tasks" Folder, you would select the "Inbox" folder).
4. Click "OK" to create the folder.

Now your "Inbox" should have a little plus sign next to it, indicating that there are subfolders available.

Changing Task List Views

In order to use Tasks effectively, it is helpful to be able to change the views. There are a few different ways to do this. The easiest way is to use the "Current View" window.

This gives you much of the information you would need and lets you quickly rank the Tasks depending on what you are looking for. For example, say you needed to know what was going on in the next week as far as your to-dos. Click on "Next Seven Days," and that is all the Task list will display. Spend some time here finding what works best for you.

Changing Database Views

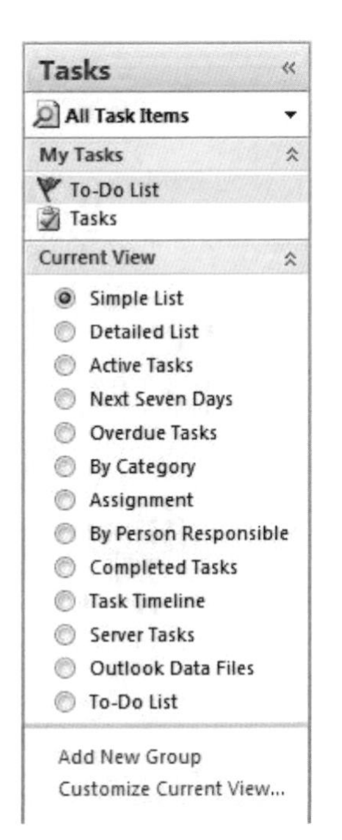

Similar to the Task list, changing the way you view your database in Outlook is helpful. Outlook usually defaults to displaying the contacts as Address Cards. Once you have more than twenty contacts, this view become confusing. Grouping the cards into categories will help you be more efficient.

While the "Current View" bar will work well, a more effective view might be to Arrange by Category. To do this:

1. Click on View at the top
2. Select Arrange By
3. Select Categories and Tasks

This breaks the categories into collapsible lists.

We use different views for different tasks; for example, when making prospecting calls, we just use the "Phone List" option from the Current View bar, and emails from the Category view.

Master Category List, Assigning Colors to Time Blocks

Creating and managing the categories is another step that can be a little confusing. This is one of the biggest differences between Outlook 2003 and Outlook 2007. The process is conceptually the same; it just looks different. In

2003, you can manage your Master Category list by going to the Edit menu, selecting Categories and then Master Category List. You will not be assigning colors to your categories in Outlook 2003.

In Outlook 2007, you can manage your Category list with just a few steps:

1. Click on your Contacts tab
2. Right-click on a category
3. Select Categorize
4. Click on the All Categories button at the bottom of the list

This will open a window that allows you to rename categories and designate colors. Spend some time going through this process, as these categories apply not only to your Contacts file, but also to the Calendar. Once this list is set, you will be able to color-code your time blocks. Review the Time Mastery chapter of this book to make sure you are selecting colors that will apply to your time blocking system. When you create a new calendar event, just click on the "Categorize" button at the top to select a color.

Mail Merges

A mail merge is a system that trickles out emails to a specific list of people. There are two main benefits:

- Most spam filters look for things such as the number of people receiving the email, the email server, etc. By trickling out the email through a mail merge, you greatly increase your chances of the email getting through the spam net.
- Secondly, by using a mail merge, you can have the email greeting personalized. This means that instead of keeping your email generic, you can write as if you were talking to one person instead of many.

There are a few steps to complete.

1. To begin, you will need to have all of your contacts already in Outlook. This means having the "Full Name" and "File As" fields complete. This is what the program uses to fill in the automatically generated "personal" greeting.
2. Once your contacts are complete, we recommend creating a distribution list. To do this,
   a. Click on File > New
   b. Select Distribution List, bringing up a new window:

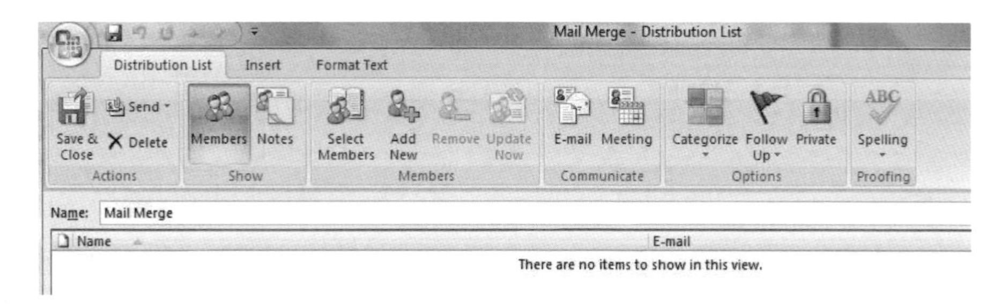

Name it whatever you like, but we recommend adding the words "Mail Merge" to it, just to keep everything clear. After naming, you can click either on the "Add New" button, or on the "Select Members" button. The "Select Members" button will open your entire contacts list, and let you select. It is a good idea to create distribution lists for your A, B, and C contacts, as well as a list for all prospects and past clients.

3. Now that you have the Distribution Lists taken care of, you will need to create a new folder so it will work with the mail merge. While in the Contacts tab, click File > New, then select Folder.

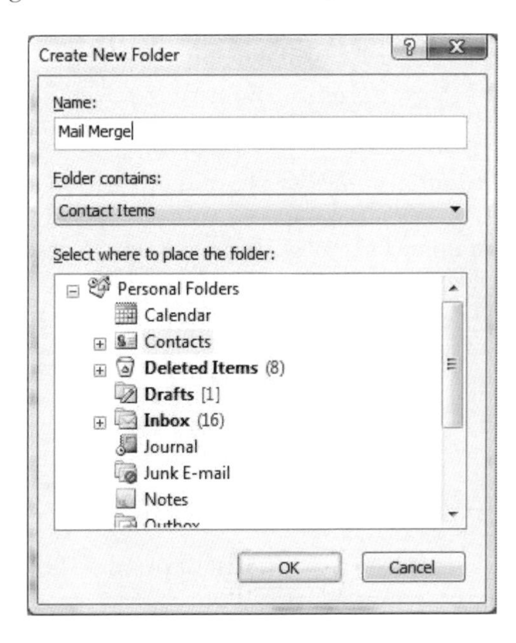

Again, give it a name. After creating the folder, it will be displayed on the left (in 2007) underneath "Contacts" as shown here:

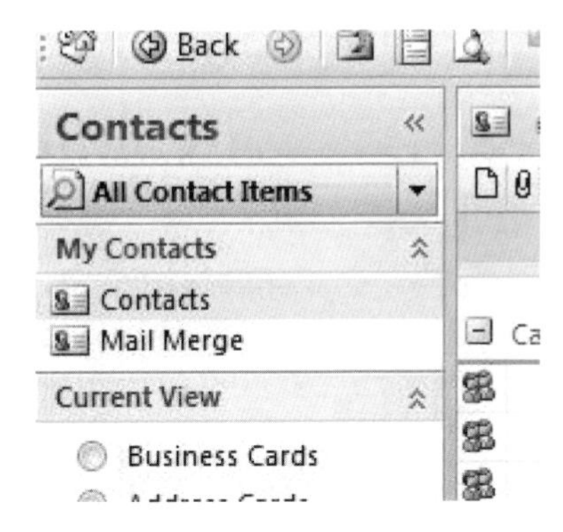

4. While on the Contacts folder, click and drag your Mail Merge **distribution list** to the appropriate folder. In this case, you would drag your **Mail Merge distribution list** to the **Mail Merge** folder.
5. Click on the Mail Merge folder, and you should see something like this:

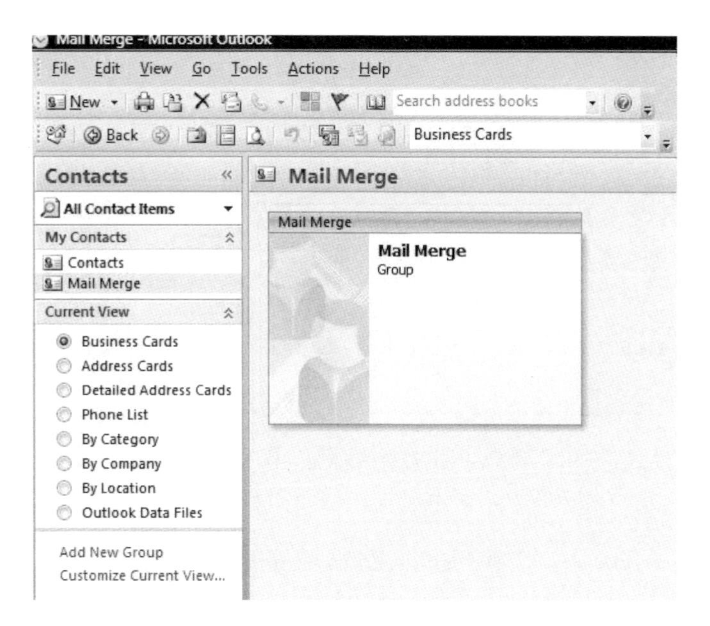

Now for the actual mail merge.

6. Open Word, and write your email. Again, keep in mind that the mail merge will fill in a greeting, so you can skip that part.
7. Once you are ready, **Save** your work (save often, by the way)
8. In Outlook 2007, click on the Mailings tab, and click on "Step by Step Mail Merge Wizard…"
9. In Outlook 2003, there is not a "Mailings" tab, but there is a Mail Merge Wizard under Tools > Letters and Mailings, then click Mail Merge.

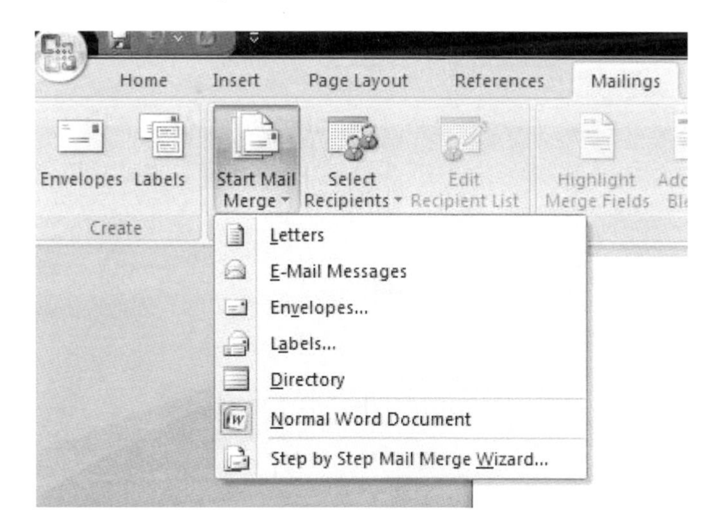

10. Once you click on the Wizard, select the "E-Mail Messages" button when it asks for the type of document.
11. When it asks for the recipients, click the "Select from Outlook contacts" button
12. Click "Choose Contacts Folder." Here is where all your tedious work from earlier on comes into play. It will display each folder you have created, so again, naming them appropriately is crucial.

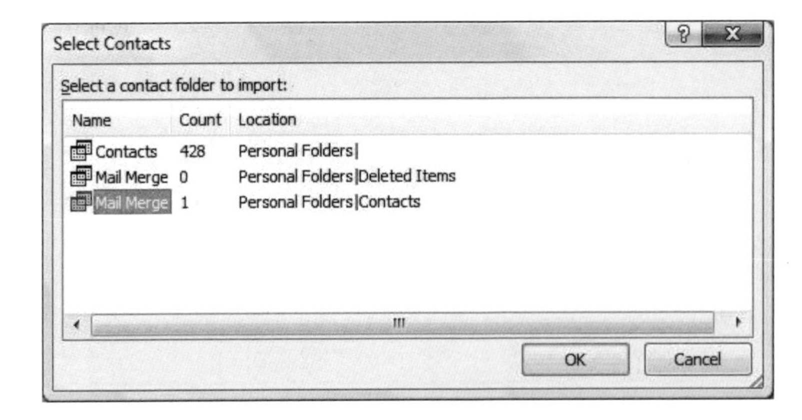

13. Click "Ok" and click the "Next" button for the Wizard. The next page will let you preview how each recipient's email will look, so tweak as needed.

Follow the next steps as requested by the Wizard, and your mail merge will be sent. Take note that because the mail merge trickles out the emails, it can take quite a while for all the emails to leave your outbox, especially if you are sending the message to a few hundred people. An urgent email that you are sending *will* get hung up until all the others are sent out. Also, shutting down your computer or exiting Outlook will leave the merge incomplete.

These are just a few functions of Outlook that are beneficial for you to know and understand if you are going to begin using Outlook as a contact manager… instead of just an email client. If you require personal assistance to apply these processes, be sure to contact us at www.EfficiencybyDesignOnline.com. We can assist you with setting up these processes, either in person or over the phone, with our network of consultants.

About the Authors

Darice Johnston has over twelve years of experience in the fields of sales, project development, writing, life coaching and business consulting.

In 2005, Darice began to establish herself as a business coach to entrepreneurs and sales professionals using the unique positioning of "efficiency expert". She knew she was on to something when she began successfully assisting her clients in achieving a more profitable sales business through the implementation of efficiency tools which she had developed and customized just for them. The dramatic results were proof enough that she had tapped into an angle of sales coaching that needed to be developed more thoroughly. She opened the doors of her company, Efficiency by Design, LLC in 2008. Darice works one on one with sales professionals and conducts seminars and retreats teaching her success series, "Unlocked: Revealing the Eight Secrets of Highly Efficient Sales Professionals."

Personal interests include reading, writing, entertaining and socializing with family and friends. As a self-proclaimed "deep sea diver of the psyche" she enjoys the study of metaphysics, quantum physics and considers herself a full-time student of Universal Law. Knowing that "success is a science", she blends in her understanding of these philosophies into her business and life coaching techniques.

Darice has established her home in Littleton, Colorado, with her daughters Andrea and Alexandra.

Lon Welsh is the founder of Your Castle Real Estate (YCRE). YCRE has 220 Realtors® and is the third largest independent (non-franchise) brokerage in metro Denver. Mr. Welsh is a very frequent speaker on topics such as sales productivity, investing and real estate trends. He frequently contributes articles on real estate trends to *The Denver Post*, the *Denver Business Journal* and the six Denver Realtor boards. He is a director at the Denver Board of Realtors. Prior to founding YCRE, Mr. Welsh spent eight years working as a consultant, first with Deloitte & Touche and later with Arthur Andersen (Accenture). At Deloitte, he managed merger and acquisition engagements. At Accenture, Mr. Welsh was a senior manager providing strategy-consulting services to high tech clients. Mr. Welsh also held several finance positions with a Fortune 100 consumer products company. He has a BBA in Finance from the University of Iowa and an MBA in Finance from Vanderbilt.

Drew Shope has been involved with social media for the past eight years. He is a Founding Partner of Thrive Social Media, LLC. He is a trainer to sales professionals on the business application of social media, Outlook, Excel, and other tools, as well as actively participating in the local blog scene. He attended Colorado State University studying Landscape Architecture, where he learned much of the web and technical skills he has used for everything from freelance web design to social media consulting.

Bruce Gardner has been licensed as a real estate Broker in Colorado since 1992. He is an Accredited Buyer's Representative, a Certified Residential Specialist and a Graduate of the Realtor® Institute. He worked with RE/MAX for 14 years and is a member of the RE/MAX Hall of Fame.

He was involved with the real estate community as a Director at the Aurora Association of Realtors® and was chosen as the 2008 Realtor® of the Year. He is currently a member of the Metrolist Board of Directors. He conducts agent training with courses such as Buyer and Seller Mastery and Lead Generation. He is employed by Your Castle Real Estate as their Director of Agent Development and does career coaching and training for the company's agents.